Forward

Our purpose for publishing the documents issued by the National Institute of Standards and Technology (NIST) is twofold. First of all, each NIST title in and of itself is very informative, however I am of the opinion that they should be looked at from the standpoint that each title is an integral part of a holistic cybersecurity strategy. Rather than look at each title just by itself, we need to look at them in groups based on how they are interrelated and designed to work together to improve cybersecurity.

For example, the group on FORENSICS security includes the following titles:

NIST SP 800-61 R 2   Computer Security Incident Handling Guide

NIST SP 800-72   Guidelines on PDA Forensics

NIST SP 800-83   Guide to Malware Incident Prevention and Handling for Desktops and Laptops

NIST SP 800-86   Guide to Integrating Forensic Techniques into Incident Response

NIST SP 800-88 R1   Guidelines for Media Sanitization

NIST SP 800-184   Guide for Cybersecurity Event Recovery

In order to assemble the entire picture of Forensics security – from what it is, how it works, what the vulnerabilities are and how to mitigate them, one must examine all of these documents. Only by going through all of them can a person understand the complete picture. Leave one of them out and you would be missing a valuable piece of the Forensics security puzzle.

Why buy a book you can download for free?

That brings me to the second reason to publish the NIST standards and that is the logistics of it all. These 7 publications consist of 771 pages. That's enough paper to fill two large three-ring binders. Nobody has a secretary anymore, so an engineer that is paid $75 an hour has to do this. The amount of time it would take an engineer to print all 7 publications (using a network printer shared with 100 other people – and it's out of paper, and the toner is low), punch holes in 771 pages and assemble the binders would easily take half a day. Our ability to deliver any NIST document quickly and efficiently is unmatched because we are printing books on demand and we are backed up by Amazon, so the titles are easy to find and simple to order. Just search Amazon.com by NIST number and you can have a copy shipped to you in a matter of days. We print all books a full 8 ½ inches by 11 inches, with large text. If there are color images in the publication, the book is probably in color, unless the color is merely decorative, in which case we print in black and white to keep the cost to you as low as possible.

Luis Ayala,
My email is cybah@webplus.net   Our website is: cybah.webplus.net
4th Watch Books is a Service Disabled Veteran Owned Small Business (SDVOSB).

CyberSecurity Standards Library™

Get a Complete Library of Over 300 Cybersecurity Standards on 1 Convenient DVD!

The **4th Watch CyberSecurity Standards Library** is a DVD disc that puts over 300 current and archived cybersecurity standards from NIST, DOD, DHS, CNSS and NERC at your fingertips! Many of these cybersecurity standards are hard to find and we included the current version and a previous version for many of them. The DVD includes four books written by Luis Ayala: **The Cyber Dictionary, Cybersecurity Standards, Cyber-Security Glossary of Building Hacks and Cyber-Attacks**, and **Cyber-Physical Attack Defenses: Preventing Damage to Buildings and Utilities**.

- ✓ DVD includes many Hard-to-find Cybersecurity Standards - some still in Draft.
- ✓ Docs are organized by source and listed numerically so each standard is easy to locate.
- ✓ The listing of standards on the DVD includes an abstract of the subject, and date issued.
- ✓ PDF format for use on PC, Mac, eReaders, or tablets.
- ✓ No need for WiFi / Internet.
- ✓ Save countless hours of searching and downloading.
- ✓ Carry in a briefcase - terrific for travel.

4th Watch Publishing is releasing the CyberSecurity Standards Library DVD to make it easier for you to access the tools you need to ensure the security of your computer networks and SCADA systems. We also publish many of these standards on demand so you don't need to waste valuable time searching for the latest version of a standard, printing hundreds of pages and punching holes so they can go in a three-ring binder. **Order on Amazon.com**

The DVD works on PC and Mac with the standards in PDF format. To view the CyberSecurity Standards Library on the DVD, a computer with a DVD drive is required. The most current version of your internet browser, at least 2GB of RAM, and current version of Adobe Reader is recommended. (Compatible browsers include Internet Explorer 8+, Mozilla Firefox 4+, Apple Safari 5+, Google Chrome 15+)

NIST Special Publication 800-18
Revision 1

Guide for Developing Security Plans for Federal Information Systems

National Institute of Standards and Technology
Technology Administration
U.S. Department of Commerce

Marianne Swanson
Joan Hash
Pauline Bowen

INFORMATION SECURITY

Computer Security Division
Information Technology Laboratory
National Institute of Standards and Technology
Gaithersburg, MD 20899-8930

February 2006

U.S. Department of Commerce
Carlos M.Gutierrez, Secretary

National Institute of Standards and Technology
William Jeffrey, Director

Reports on Information Systems Technology

The Information Technology Laboratory (ITL) at the National Institute of Standards and Technology promotes the United States economy and public welfare by providing technical leadership for the Nation's measurement and standards infrastructure. ITL develops tests, test methods, reference data, proof-of-concept implementations, and technical analyses to advance the development and productive use of information technology. ITL's responsibilities include the development of management, administrative, technical, and physical standards and guidelines for the cost-effective security and privacy of non-national-security-related information in federal information systems. This Special Publication 800 series reports on ITL's research, guidelines, and outreach efforts in information system security and its collaborative activities with industry, government, and academic organizations.

Authority

This document has been developed by the National Institute of Standards and Technology (NIST) in furtherance of its statutory responsibilities under the Federal Information Security Management Act of 2002, Public Law 107-347.

NIST is responsible for developing standards and guidelines, including minimum requirements, for providing adequate information security for all agency operations and assets, but such standards and guidelines shall not apply to national security systems. This guideline is consistent with the requirements of the Office of Management and Budget (OMB) Circular A-130, Section 8b(3), Securing Agency Information Systems, as analyzed in A-130, Appendix IV: Analysis of Key Sections. Supplemental information is provided in A-130, Appendix III.

This guideline has been prepared for use by federal agencies. It may be used by nongovernmental organizations on a voluntary basis and is not subject to copyright. (Attribution would be appreciated by NIST.)

Nothing in this document should be taken to contradict standards and guidelines made mandatory and binding on federal agencies by the Secretary of Commerce under statutory authority. Nor should these guidelines be interpreted as altering or superseding the existing authorities of the Secretary of Commerce, Director of the OMB, or any other federal official.

Certain commercial entities, equipment, or materials may be identified in this document in order to describe an experimental procedure or concept adequately. Such identification is not intended to imply recommendation or endorsement by the National Institute of Standards and Technology, nor is it intended to imply that the entities, materials, or equipment are necessarily the best available for the purpose.

Acknowledgements

The National Institute of Standards and Technology would like to acknowledge the authors of the original NIST Special Publication 800-18, *Guide for Developing Security Plans for Information Technology System.* The original document was used as the foundation for this revision. Additionally, thank you to all the NIST staff that reviewed and commented on the document.

Table of Contents

Executive Summary

The objective of system security planning is to improve protection of information system resources. All federal systems have some level of sensitivity and require protection as part of good management practice. The protection of a system must be documented in a system security plan. The completion of system security plans is a requirement of the Office of Management and Budget (OMB) Circular A-130, "Management of Federal Information Resources," Appendix III, "Security of Federal Automated Information Resources," and" Title III of the E-Government Act, entitled the Federal Information Security Management Act (FISMA).

The purpose of the system security plan is to provide an overview of the security requirements of the system and describe the controls in place or planned for meeting those requirements. The system security plan also delineates responsibilities and expected behavior of all individuals who access the system. The system security plan should be viewed as documentation of the structured process of planning adequate, cost-effective security protection for a system. It should reflect input from various managers with responsibilities concerning the system, including information owners, the system owner, and the senior agency information security officer (SAISO). Additional information may be included in the basic plan and the structure and format organized according to agency needs, so long as the major sections described in this document are adequately covered and readily identifiable.

In order for the plans to adequately reflect the protection of the resources, a senior management official must authorize a system to operate. The authorization of a system to process information, granted by a management official, provides an important quality control. By authorizing processing in a system, the manager accepts its associated risk.

Management authorization should be based on an assessment of management, operational, and technical controls. Since the system security plan establishes and documents the security controls, it should form the basis for the authorization, supplemented by the assessment report and the plan of actions and milestones. In addition, a periodic review of controls should also contribute to future authorizations. Re-authorization should occur whenever there is a significant change in processing, but at least every three years.

1. Introduction

Today's rapidly changing technical environment requires federal agencies to adopt a minimum set of security controls to protect their information and information systems. Federal Information Processing Standard (FIPS) 200, *Minimum Security Requirements for Federal Information and Information Systems*, specifies the minimum security requirements for federal information and information systems in seventeen security-related areas. Federal agencies must meet the minimum security requirements defined in FIPS 200 through the use of the security controls in NIST Special Publication 800-53, *Recommended Security Controls for Federal Information Systems*. NIST SP 800-53 contains the management, operational, and technical safeguards or countermeasures prescribed for an information system. The controls selected or planned must be documented in a system security plan. This document provides guidance for federal agencies for developing system security plans for federal information systems.

1.1 Background

Title III of the E-Government Act, entitled the Federal Information Security Management Act (FISMA), requires each federal agency to develop, document, and implement an agency-wide information security program to provide information security for the information and information systems that support the operations and assets of the agency, including those provided or managed by another agency, contractor, or other source. System security planning is an important activity that supports the system development life cycle (SDLC) and should be updated as system events trigger the need for revision in order to accurately reflect the most current state of the system. The system security plan provides a summary of the security requirements for the information system and describes the security controls in place or planned for meeting those requirements. The plan also may reference other key security-related documents for the information system such as a risk assessment, plan of action and milestones, accreditation decision letter, privacy impact assessment, contingency plan, configuration management plan, security configuration checklists, and system interconnection agreements as appropriate.

1.2 Target Audience

Program managers, system owners, and security personnel in the organization must understand the system security planning process. In addition, users of the information system and those responsible for defining system requirements should be familiar with the system security planning process. Those responsible for implementing and managing information systems must participate in addressing security controls to be applied to their systems. This guidance provides basic information on how to prepare a system security plan and is designed to be adaptable in a variety of organizational structures and used as reference by those having assigned responsibility for activity related to security planning.

1.3 Organization of Document

This publication introduces a set of activities and concepts to develop an information system security plan. A brief description of its contents follows:

- ***Chapter 1*** includes background information relevant to the system security planning process, target audience, information on FIPS 199, *Standards for Security Categorization of Federal Information and Information Systems*, a discussion of the various categories of information systems, identification of related NIST publications, and a description of the roles and responsibilities related to the development of system security plans.
- ***Chapter 2*** discusses how agencies should analyze their information system inventories in the process of establishing system boundaries. It also discusses identification of common security controls and scoping guidance.
- ***Chapter 3*** takes the reader through the steps of system security plan development.
- ***Appendix A*** provides a system security plan template.
- ***Appendix B*** provides a glossary of terms and definitions.
- ***Appendix C*** includes references that support this publication.

1.4 Systems Inventory and Federal Information Processing Standards (FIPS 199)

FISMA requires that agencies have in place an information systems inventory. All information systems in the inventory should be categorized using FIPS 199 as a first step in the system security planning activity.

FIPS 199 is the mandatory standard to be used by all federal agencies to categorize all information and information systems collected or maintained by or on behalf of each agency based on the objectives of providing appropriate levels of information security according to impact. Security categorization standards for information and information systems provide a common framework and understanding for expressing security that, for the federal government, promotes: (i) effective management and oversight of information security programs, including the coordination of information security efforts throughout the civilian, national security, emergency preparedness, homeland security, and law enforcement communities; and (ii) consistent reporting to the Office of Management and Budget (OMB) and Congress on the adequacy and effectiveness of information security policies, procedures, and practices.

1.5 Major Applications, General Support Systems, and Minor Applications

All information systems must be covered by a system security plan and labeled as a major application[1] or general support system.[2]   Specific system security plans for minor

---

[1] OMB Circular A-130, Appendix III, defines major application as an application that requires special attention to security due to the risk and magnitude of harm resulting from the loss, misuse, or unauthorized access to or modification of the information in the application.

[2] OMB Circular A-130, Appendix III, defines general support system as an interconnected set of information resources under the same direct management control that shares common functionality. It normally includes hardware, software, information, data, applications, communications, and people.

applications[3] are not required because the security controls for those applications are typically provided by the general support system or major application in which they operate. In those cases where the minor application is not connected to a major application or general support system, the minor application should be briefly described in a general support system plan that has either a common physical location or is supported by the same organization. Additional information is provided in Chapter 2.

1.6 Other Related NIST Publications

In order to develop the system security plan, it is necessary to be familiar with NIST security standards and guidelines. It is essential that users of this publication understand the requirements and methodology for information system categorization as described in NIST FIPS 199 as well as the requirements for addressing minimum security controls for a given system as described in NIST SP 800-53, *Recommended Security Controls for Federal Information Systems,* and FIPS 200, *Minimum Security Requirements for Federal information and Information System.*

Other key NIST publications directly supporting the preparation of the security plan are NIST SP 800-30, *Risk Management Guide for Information Technology Systems,* and NIST SP 800-37, *Guide for the Security Certification and Accreditation of Federal Information Systems.* All documents can be obtained from the NIST Computer Security Resource Center website at: http://csrc.nist.gov/.

1.7 System Security Plan Responsibilities

Agencies should develop policy on the system security planning process. System security plans are living documents that require periodic review, modification, and plans of action and milestones for implementing security controls. Procedures should be in place outlining who reviews the plans, keeps the plan current, and follows up on planned security controls. In addition, procedures should require that system security plans be developed and reviewed prior to proceeding with the security certification and accreditation process for the system.

During the security certification and accreditation process, the system security plan is analyzed, updated, and accepted. The certification agent confirms that the security controls described in the system security plan are consistent with the FIPS 199 security category determined for the information system, and that the threat and vulnerability identification and initial risk determination are identified and documented in the system security plan, risk assessment, or equivalent document. The results of a security certification are used to reassess the risks, develop the plan of action and milestones (POA&Ms) which are required to track remedial actions, and update the system security plan, thus providing the factual basis for an authorizing official to render a security

---

[3] NIST Special Publication 800-37 defines a minor application as an application, other than a major application, that requires attention to security due to the risk and magnitude of harm resulting from the loss, misuse, or unauthorized access to or modification of the information in the application. Minor applications are typically included as part of a general support system.

accreditation decision. For additional information on the certification and accreditation process, see NIST SP 800-37. Figure 1, depicts the key inputs/outputs into the security planning process.

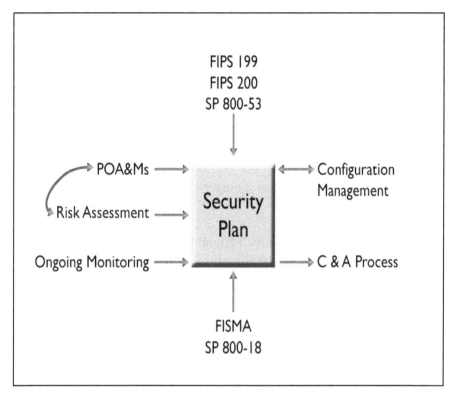

Figure 1: Security Planning Process Inputs/Outputs

The roles and responsibilities in this section are specific to information system security planning. Recognizing that agencies have widely varying missions and organizational structures, there may be differences in naming conventions for security planning-related roles and how the associated responsibilities are allocated among agency personnel (e.g., multiple individuals filling a single role or one individual filling multiple roles[4]).

1.7.1 Chief Information Officer

The Chief Information Officer (CIO)[5] is the agency official responsible for developing and maintaining an agency-wide information security program and has the following responsibilities for system security planning:

- Designates a senior agency information security officer (SAISO) who shall carry out the CIO's responsibilities for system security planning,

---

[4] Caution should be exercised when one individual fills multiple roles in the security planning process to ensure that the individual retains an appropriate level of independence and remains free from conflicts of interest.

[5] When an agency has not designated a formal CIO position, FISMA requires the associated responsibilities to be handled by a comparable agency official.

- Develops and maintains information security policies, procedures, and control techniques to address system security planning,

- Manages the identification, implementation, and assessment of common security controls,

- Ensures that personnel with significant responsibilities for system security plans are trained,

- Assists senior agency officials with their responsibilities for system security plans, and

- Identifies and coordinates common security controls for the agency.

1.7.2 Information System Owner

The information system owner[6] is the agency official responsible for the overall procurement, development, integration, modification, or operation and maintenance of the information system. The information system owner has the following responsibilities related to system security plans:

- Develops the system security plan in coordination with information owners, the system administrator, the information system security officer, the senior agency information security officer, and functional "end users,"

- Maintains the system security plan and ensures that the system is deployed and operated according to the agreed-upon security requirements,

- Ensures that system users and support personnel receive the requisite security training (e.g., instruction in rules of behavior),

- Updates the system security plan whenever a significant change occurs, and

- Assists in the identification, implementation, and assessment of the common security controls.

1.7.3 Information Owner

The information owner is the agency official with statutory or operational authority for specified information and responsibility for establishing the controls for its generation, collection, processing, dissemination, and disposal. The information owner has the following responsibilities related to system security plans:

---

[6] The role of the information system owner can be interpreted in a variety of ways depending on the particular agency and the system development life cycle phase of the information system. Some agencies may refer to information system owners as program managers or business/asset/mission owners.

- Establishes the rules for appropriate use and protection of the subject data/information (rules of behavior),[7]

- Provides input to information system owners regarding the security requirements and security controls for the information system(s) where the information resides,

- Decides who has access to the information system and with what types of privileges or access rights, and

- Assists in the identification and assessment of the common security controls where the information resides.

1.7.4 Senior Agency Information Security Officer (SAISO)

The senior agency information security officer is the agency official responsible for serving as the CIO's primary liaison to the agency's information system owners and information system security officers. The SAISO has the following responsibilities related to system security plans:

- Carries out the CIO's responsibilities for system security planning,

- Coordinates the development, review, and acceptance of system security plans with information system owners, information system security officers, and the authorizing official,

- Coordinates the identification, implementation, and assessment of the common security controls, and

- Possesses professional qualifications, including training and experience, required to develop and review system security plans.

1.7.5 Information System Security Officer

The information system security officer is the agency official assigned responsibility by the SAISO, authorizing official, management official, or information system owner for ensuring that the appropriate operational security posture is maintained for an information system or program. The information system security officer has the following responsibilities related to system security plans:

- Assists the senior agency information security officer in the identification, implementation, and assessment of the common security controls, and

---

[7] The information owner retains that responsibility even when the data/information are shared with other organizations.

- Plays an active role in developing and updating the system security plan as well as coordinating with the information system owner any changes to the system and assessing the security impact of those changes.

1.7.6 Authorizing Official

The authorizing official (or designated approving/accrediting authority as referred to by some agencies) is a senior management official or executive with the authority to formally assume responsibility for operating an information system at an acceptable level of risk to agency operations, agency assets, or individuals.[8] The authorizing official has the following responsibilities related to system security plans:

- Approves system security plans,

- Authorizes operation of an information system,

- Issues an interim authorization to operate the information system under specific terms and conditions, or

- Denies authorization to operate the information system (or if the system is already operational, halts operations) if unacceptable security risks exist.

1.8 Rules of Behavior

The rules of behavior, which are required in OMB Circular A-130, Appendix III, and is a security control contained in NIST SP 800-53, should clearly delineate responsibilities and expected behavior of all individuals with access to the system. The rules should state the consequences of inconsistent behavior or noncompliance and be made available to every user prior to receiving authorization for access to the system. It is required that the rules contain a signature page for each user to acknowledge receipt, indicating that they have read, understand, and agree to abide by the rules of behavior. Electronic signatures are acceptable for use in acknowledging the rules of behavior.

Figure 2 lists examples from OMB Circular A-130 Appendix III of what should be covered in typical rules of behavior. These are examples only and agencies have flexibility in the detail and contents. When developing the rules of behavior, keep in mind that the intent is to make all users accountable for their actions by acknowledging that they have read, understand, and agree to abide by the rules of behavior. The rules should not be a complete copy of the security policy or procedures guide, but rather cover, at a high level, some of the controls described in the following Figure.

---

[8] In some agencies, the senior official and the Chief Information Officer may be co-authorizing officials. In this situation, the senior official approves the operation of the information system prior to the Chief Information Officer.

Examples of Controls Contained in Rules of Behavior

- Delineate responsibilities, expected use of system, and behavior of all users.
- Describe appropriate limits on interconnections.
- Define service provisions and restoration priorities.
- Describe consequences of behavior not consistent with rules.
- Covers the following topics:
  - Work at home
  - Dial-in access
  - Connection to the Internet
  - Use of copyrighted work
  - Unofficial use of government equipment
  - Assignment and limitations of system privileges and individual accountability
  - Password usage
  - Searching databases and divulging information.

Figure 2: Rules of Behavior Examples

1.9 System Security Plan Approval

Organizational policy should clearly define who is responsible for system security plan approval and procedures developed for plan submission, including any special memorandum language or other documentation required by the agency. Prior to the certification and accreditation process, the designated Authorizing Official, independent from the system owner, typically approves the plan.

2. System Boundary Analysis and Security Controls

Before the system security plan can be developed, the information system and the information resident within that system must be categorized based on a FIPS 199 impact analysis. Then a determination can be made as to which systems in the inventory can be logically grouped into major applications or general support systems. The FIPS 199 impact levels must be considered when the system boundaries are drawn and when selecting the initial set of security controls (i.e., control baseline). The baseline security controls can then be tailored based on an assessment of risk and local conditions including organization-specific security requirements, specific threat information, cost-benefit analyses, the availability of compensating controls, or special circumstances. Common security controls, which is one of the tailoring considerations, must be identified prior to system security plan preparation in order to identity those controls covered at the agency level, which are not system-specific. These common security controls can then be incorporated into the system security plan by reference.

2.1 System Boundaries

The process of uniquely assigning information resources[9] to an information system defines the security boundary for that system. Agencies have great flexibility in determining what constitutes an information system (i.e., major application or general support system). If a set of information resources is identified as an information system, the resources should generally be under the same direct management control. Direct management control[10] does not necessarily imply that there is no intervening management. It is also possible for an information system to contain multiple *subsystems*.

A subsystem is a major subdivision or component of an information system consisting of information, information technology, and personnel that perform one or more specific functions. Subsystems typically fall under the same management authority and are included within a single system security plan. Figure 3 depicts a general support system with three subsystems.

In addition to the consideration of direct management control, it may be helpful for agencies to consider if the information resources being identified as an information system:

- Have the same function or mission objective and essentially the same operating characteristics and security needs, and

---

[9] Information resources consist of information and related resources, such as personnel, equipment, funds, and information technology.

[10] Direct management control typically involves budgetary, programmatic, or operational authority and associated responsibility. For new information systems, management control can be interpreted as having budgetary/programmatic authority and responsibility for the development and deployment of the information systems. For information systems currently in the federal inventory, management control can be interpreted as having budgetary/operational authority for the day-to-day operations and maintenance of the information systems.

- Reside in the same general operating environment (or in the case of a distributed information system, reside in various locations with similar operating environments).

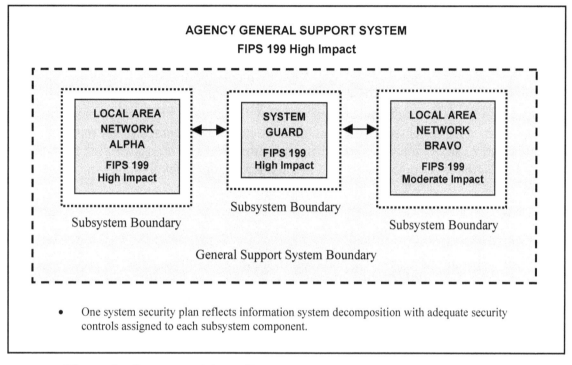

Figure 3: Decomposition of large and complex information systems

While the above considerations may be useful to agencies in determining information system boundaries for purposes of security accreditation, they should not be viewed as limiting the agency's flexibility in establishing boundaries that promote effective information security within the available resources of the agency. Authorizing officials and senior agency information security officers should consult with prospective information system owners when establishing information system boundaries. The process of establishing boundaries for agency information systems and the associated security implications, is an agency-level activity that should include careful negotiation among all key participants—taking into account the mission/business requirements of the agency, the technical considerations with respect to information security, and the programmatic costs to the agency.

FIPS 199 defines security categories for information systems based on potential impact on organizations, assets, or individuals should there be a breach of security—that is, a loss of confidentiality, integrity, or availability. FIPS 199 security categories can play an important part in defining information system boundaries by partitioning the agency's information systems according to the criticality or sensitivity of the information and information systems and the importance of those systems in accomplishing the agency's mission. This is particularly important when there are various FIPS 199 impact levels contained in one information system. The FIPS 199 requirement to secure an information system to the high watermark or highest impact level must be applied when grouping minor applications/subsystems with varying FIPS 199 impact levels into a single general support system or major application unless there is adequate boundary protection, e.g., firewalls and encryption, around those subsystems or applications with the highest impact level. Additionally, there must be assurance that the shared resources, i.e., networks, communications, and physical access within the whole general support system or major application, are protected adequately for the highest impact level. Having the ability to isolate the high impact systems will not only result in more secure systems, but will also reduce the amount of resources required to secure many applications/systems that do not require that level of security. NIST SP 800-53 provides three security control baselines, i.e., low, moderate, and high, that are associated with the three FIPS 199 impact levels; as the impact level increases, so do the minimum assurance requirements. For reporting purposes, i.e., FISMA annual report, when an information system has varying FIPS 199 impact levels, that system is categorized at the highest impact level on that information system.

2.2 Major Applications

All federal applications have value and require some level of protection. Certain applications, because of the information they contain, process, store, or transmit, or because of their criticality to the agency's mission, require special management oversight. These applications are major applications. A major application is expected to have a FIPS 199 impact level of moderate or high. OMB Circular A-130 defines a "major information system" as an information system that requires special management attention because of its importance to an agency mission; its high development, operating, or maintenance costs; or its significant role in the administration of agency programs, finances, property, or other resources. Major applications are by definition major information systems.

Major applications are systems that perform clearly defined functions for which there are readily identifiable security considerations and needs (e.g., an electronic funds transfer system). A major application might comprise many individual programs and hardware, software, and telecommunications components. These components can be a single software application or a combination of hardware/software focused on supporting a specific, mission-related function. A major application may also consist of multiple individual applications if all are related to a single mission function (e.g., payroll or personnel). If a system is defined as a major application and the application is run on another organization's general support system, the major application owner is responsible for acceptance of risk and in addition:

- Notifies the general support system owner that the application is critical and provides specific security requirements;

- Provides a copy of the major application's system security plan to the operator of the general support system;

- Requests a copy of the system security plan of the general support system and ensures that it provides adequate protection for the application and information; and

- Includes a reference to the general support system security plan in the major application system security plan.

2.3 General Support Systems

A general support system is an interconnected set of information resources under the same direct management control that shares common functionality. A general support system normally includes hardware, software, information, data, applications, communications, facilities, and people and provides support for a variety of users and/or applications. A general support system, for example[11], can be a:

- LAN including smart terminals that support a branch office;
- Backbone (e.g., agency-wide);
- Communications network;
- Agency data processing center including its operating system and utilities,
- Tactical radio network; or
- Shared information processing service facility

A general support system can have a FIPS 199 impact level of low, moderate, or high in its security categorization depending on the criticality or sensitivity of the system and any major applications the general support system is supporting. A general support system is considered a major information system when special management attention is required, there are high development, operating, or maintenance costs; and the system/information has a significant role in the administration of agency programs. When the general support system is a major information system, the system's FIPS 199 impact level is either moderate or high.

A major application can be hosted on a general support system. The general support system plan should reference the major application system security plan.

2.4 Minor Applications

Agencies are expected to exercise management judgment in determining which of their applications are minor applications and to ensure that the security requirements of minor applications are addressed as part of the system security plan for the applicable general support systems or, in some cases, the applicable major application. It is very common that a minor application may have a majority of its security controls provided by the general support system or major application on which it resides. If this is the case, the information system owner of the general support system or major application is the information system owner for the minor application and is responsible for developing the

---

[11] The example provided is a small sampling of general support systems; it is not a definitive list.

system security plan. The additional security controls specific to the minor application should be documented in the system security plan as an appendix or paragraph. The minor application owner (often the same as information owner) may develop the appendix or paragraph describing the additional controls. The complete general support system or major application system security plan should be shared with the information owner.

The minor application can have a FIPS 199 security category of low or moderate. However, if the minor application resides on a system that does not have adequate boundary protection, the minor application must implement the minimum baseline controls required by the host or interconnected system.

2.5 Security Controls

FIPS 200 provides seventeen minimum security requirements for federal information and information systems. The requirements represent a broad-based, balanced information security program that addresses the management, operational, and technical aspects of protecting the confidentiality, integrity, and availability of federal information and information systems. An agency must meet the minimum security requirements in this standard by applying security controls selected in accordance with NIST SP 800-53 and the designated impact levels of the information systems. An agency has the flexibility to tailor the security control baseline in accordance with the terms and conditions set forth in the standard. Tailoring activities include: (i) the application of scoping guidance; (ii) the specification of compensating controls; and (iii) the specification of agency-defined parameters in the security controls, where allowed. The system security plan should document all tailoring activities.

2.5.1 Scoping Guidance

Scoping guidance provides an agency with specific terms and conditions on the applicability and implementation of individual security controls in the security control baselines defined in NIST SP 800-53. Several considerations described below can potentially impact how the baseline security controls are applied by the agency. System security plans should clearly identify which security controls employed scoping guidance and include a description of the type of considerations that were made. The application of scoping guidance must be reviewed and approved by the authorizing official for the information system.

Technology-related considerations—

- Security controls that refer to specific technologies (e.g., wireless, cryptography, public key infrastructure) will only be applicable if those technologies are employed or are required to be employed within the information system.

- Security controls will only be applicable to those components of the information system that typically provide the security capability addressed by the minimum security requirements.

- Security controls that can be either explicitly or implicitly supported by automated mechanisms will not require the development of such mechanisms if the mechanisms do not already exist or are not readily available in commercial or government off-the-shelf products. In situations where automated mechanisms are not readily available or technically feasible, compensating security controls, implemented through non-automated mechanisms or procedures, will be used to satisfy minimum security requirements.

Common security control-related considerations—

- Security controls designated by the agency as common controls will, in most cases, be managed by an organizational entity other than the information system owner. Every control in a security control baseline must be addressed either by the agency through common security controls or by the information system owner. Decisions on common control designations must not, however, affect the agency's responsibility in providing the necessary security controls required to meet the minimum security requirements for the information system. (Additional information on common controls is provided in Section 2.5.3.)

Public access information systems-related considerations—

- Security controls associated with public access information systems must be carefully considered and applied with discretion since some of the security controls from the specified security control baselines (e.g., personnel security controls, identification and authentication controls) may not be applicable to users accessing information systems through public interfaces.[12]

Infrastructure-related considerations—

- Security controls that refer to agency facilities (e.g., physical access controls such as locks and guards, environmental controls for temperature, humidity, lighting, fire, and power) will be applicable only to those sections of the facilities that directly provide protection to, support for, or are related to the information system (including its information technology assets such as electronic mail or web servers, server farms, data centers, networking nodes, controlled interface equipment, and communications equipment).

---

[12] For example, while the baseline security controls require identification and authentication of organizational personnel who maintain and support information systems that provide public access services, the same controls might not be required for users accessing those systems through public interfaces to obtain publicly available information. On the other hand, identification and authentication must be required for users accessing information systems through public interfaces to access their private/personal information.

Scalability-related considerations—

-      Security controls will be scalable by the size and complexity of the particular agency implementing the controls and the impact level of the information system. Scalability addresses the breadth and depth of security control implementation. Discretion is needed in scaling the security controls to the particular environment of use to ensure a cost-effective, risk-based approach to security control implementation.[13]

Risk-related considerations—

-      Security controls that uniquely support the confidentiality, integrity, or availability security objectives can be downgraded to the corresponding control in a lower baseline (or appropriately modified or eliminated if not defined in a lower baseline) if, and only if, the downgrading action: (i) is consistent with the FIPS 199 security categorization for the corresponding security objectives of confidentiality, integrity, or availability before moving to the high watermark;[14] (ii) is supported by an agency's assessment of risk; and (iii) does not affect the security-relevant information within the information system.[15]

2.5.2 Compensating Controls

Compensating security controls are the management, operational, or technical controls employed by an agency in lieu of prescribed controls in the low, moderate, or high security control baselines, which provide equivalent or comparable protection for an information system. Compensating security controls for an information system will be employed by an agency only under the following conditions: (i) the agency selects the compensating controls from the security control catalog in NIST SP 800-53; (ii) the agency provides a complete and convincing rationale and justification for how the compensating controls provide an equivalent security capability or level of protection for the information system; and (iii) the agency assesses and formally accepts the risk associated with employing the compensating controls in the information system. The use

---

[13] For example, a contingency plan for a large and complex organization with a moderate-impact or high-impact information system may be quite lengthy and contain a significant amount of implementation detail. In contrast, a contingency plan for a smaller organization with a low-impact information system may be considerably shorter and contain much less implementation detail.

[14] When employing the "high watermark" concept, some of the security objectives (i.e., confidentiality, integrity, or availability) may have been increased to a higher impact level. As such, the security controls that uniquely support these security objectives will have been upgraded as well. Consequently, organizations must consider appropriate and allowable downgrading actions to ensure cost-effective, risk-based application of security controls.

[15] Information that is security-relevant at the system level (e.g., password files, network routing tables, cryptographic key management information) must be distinguished from user-level information within an information system. Certain security controls within an information system are used to support the security objectives of confidentiality and integrity for both user-level and system-level information. Organizations must exercise caution in downgrading confidentiality or integrity-related security controls to ensure that the downgrading action does not affect the security-relevant information within the information system.

of compensating security controls must be reviewed, documented in the system security plan, and approved by the authorizing official for the information system.

2.5.3 Common Security Controls

An agency-wide view of the information security program facilitates the identification of common security controls that can be applied to one or more agency information systems. Common security controls can apply to: (i) all agency information systems; (ii) a group of information systems at a specific site (sometimes associated with the terms site certification/accreditation); or (iii) common information systems, subsystems, or applications (i.e., common hardware, software, and/or firmware) deployed at multiple operational sites (sometimes associated with the terms type certification/accreditation). Common security controls, typically identified during a collaborative agency-wide process with the involvement of the CIO, SAISO, authorizing officials, information system owners, and information system security officers (and by developmental program managers in the case of common security controls for common hardware, software, and/or firmware), have the following properties:

- The development, implementation, and assessment of common security controls can be assigned to responsible agency officials or organizational elements (other than the information system owners whose systems will implement or use those common security controls); and

- The results from the assessment of the common security controls can be used to support the security certification and accreditation processes of agency information systems where those controls have been applied.

Many of the management and operational controls (e.g., contingency planning controls, incident response controls, security awareness and training controls, personnel security controls, and physical security controls) needed to protect an information system may be excellent candidates for common security control status. The objective is to reduce security costs by centrally managing the development, implementation, and assessment of the common security controls designated by the agency—and subsequently, sharing assessment results with the owners of information systems where those common security controls are applied. Security controls not designated as common controls are considered *system-specific controls* and are the responsibility of the information system owner. System security plans should clearly identify which security controls have been designated as common security controls and which controls have been designated as system-specific controls.

For efficiency in developing system security plans, common security controls should be documented once and then inserted or imported into each system security plan for the information systems within the agency. The individual responsible for implementing the common control should be listed in the security plan. Effectively maximizing the application of common controls in the system security planning process depends upon the following factors:

- The agency has developed, documented, and communicated its specific guidance on identifying common security controls;

- The agency has assigned the responsibility for coordinating common security control identification and review and obtaining consensus on the common control designations, to a management official with security program responsibilities such as the CIO or SAISO;

- System owners have been briefed on the system security planning process including use of common controls; and

- Agency experts in the common control areas identified have been consulted as part of the process.

An agency may also assign a hybrid status to security controls in situations where one part of the control is deemed to be common, while another part of the control is deemed to be system-specific. For example, an agency may view the IR-1 (Incident Response Policy and Procedures) security control as a hybrid control with the policy portion of the control deemed to be common and the procedures portion of the control deemed to be system-specific. Hybrid security controls may also serve as templates for further control refinement. An agency may choose, for example, to implement the CP-2 (Contingency Plan) security control as a master template for a generalized contingency plan for all agency information systems with individual information system owners tailoring the plan, where appropriate, for system-specific issues.

Information system owners are responsible for any system-specific issues associated with the implementation of an agency's common security controls. These issues are identified and described in the system security plans for the individual information systems. The SAISO, acting on behalf of the CIO, should coordinate with agency officials (e.g., facilities managers, site managers, personnel managers) responsible for the development and implementation of the designated common security controls to ensure that the required controls are put into place, the controls are assessed, and the assessment results are shared with the appropriate information system owners.

Partitioning security controls into common security controls and system-specific security controls can result in significant savings to the agency in control development and implementation costs. It can also result in a more consistent application of the security controls across the agency at large. Moreover, equally significant savings can be realized in the security certification and accreditation process. Rather than assessing common security controls in every information system, the certification process draws upon any applicable results from the most current assessment of the common security controls performed at the agency level. An agency-wide approach to reuse and sharing of assessment results can greatly enhance the efficiency of the security certifications and accreditations being conducted by an agency and significantly reduce security program costs.

While the concept of security control partitioning into common security controls and system-specific controls is straightforward and intuitive, the application of this principle within an agency takes planning, coordination, and perseverance. If an agency is just beginning to implement this approach or has only partially implemented this approach, it may take some time to get the maximum benefits from security control partitioning and the associated reuse of assessment evidence. Because of the potential dependence on common security controls by many of an agency's information systems, a failure of such common controls may result in a significant increase in agency-level risk—risk that arises from the operation of the systems that depend on these controls.

3. Plan Development

The remainder of this document guides the reader in writing a system security plan, including logical steps which should be followed in approaching plan development, recommended structure and content, and how to maximize the use of current NIST publications to effectively support system security planning activity. There should be established agency policy on how the information system security plans are to be controlled and accessed prior to initiation of the activity.

3.1 System Name and Identifier

The first item listed in the system security plan is the system name and identifier. As required in OMB Circular A-11, each system should be assigned a name and unique identifier. Assignment of a unique identifier supports the agency's ability to easily collect agency information and security metrics specific to the system as well as facilitate complete traceability to all requirements related to system implementation and performance. This identifier should remain the same throughout the life of the system and be retained in audit logs related to system use.

3.2 System Categorization

Each system identified in the agency's system inventory must be categorized using FIPS 199. NIST Special Publication 800-60, *Guide for Mapping Types of Information and Information Systems to Security Categories,* provides implementation guidance in completing this activity. See Table 1 for a summary of FIPS 199 categories.

3.3 System Owner

A designated system owner must be identified in the system security plan for each system. This person is the key point of contact (POC) for the system and is responsible for coordinating system development life cycle (SDLC) activities specific to the system. It is important that this person have expert knowledge of the system capabilities and functionality. The assignment of a system owner should be documented in writing and the plan should include the following contact information:

- Name
- Title
- Agency
- Address
- Phone Number
- Email Address

Security Objective	POTENTIAL IMPACT		
	LOW	MODERATE	HIGH
Confidentiality Preserving authorized restrictions on information access and disclosure, including means for protecting personal privacy and proprietary information. [44 U.S.C., SEC. 3542]	The unauthorized disclosure of information could be expected to have a **limited** adverse effect on organizational operations, organizational assets, or individuals.	The unauthorized disclosure of information could be expected to have a **serious** adverse effect on organizational operations, organizational assets, or individuals.	The unauthorized disclosure of information could be expected to have a **severe or catastrophic** adverse effect on organizational operations, organizational assets, or individuals.
Integrity Guarding against improper information modification or destruction, and includes ensuring information non-repudiation and authenticity. [44 U.S.C., SEC. 3542]	The unauthorized modification or destruction of information could be expected to have a **limited** adverse effect on organizational operations, organizational assets, or individuals.	The unauthorized modification or destruction of information could be expected to have a **serious** adverse effect on organizational operations, organizational assets, or individuals.	The unauthorized modification or destruction of information could be expected to have a **severe or catastrophic** adverse effect on organizational operations, organizational assets, or individuals.
Availability Ensuring timely and reliable access to and use of information. [44 U.S.C., SEC. 3542]	The disruption of access to or use of information or an information system could be expected to have a **limited** adverse effect on organizational operations, organizational assets, or individuals.	The disruption of access to or use of information or an information system could be expected to have a **serious** adverse effect on organizational operations, organizational assets, or individuals.	The disruption of access to or use of information or an information system could be expected to have a **severe or catastrophic** adverse effect on organizational operations, organizational assets, or individuals.

Table 1: FIPS 199 Categorization

3.4 Authorizing Official

An authorizing official must be identified in the system security plan for each system. This person is the senior management official who has the authority to authorize operation (accredit) of an information system (major application or general support system) and accept the residual risk associated with the system. The assignment of the authorizing official should be in writing, and the plan must include the same contact information listed in Section 3.3.

3.5 Other Designated Contacts

This section should include names of other key contact personnel who can address inquiries regarding system characteristics and operation. The same information listed in Section 3.3 should be included for each person listed under this section.

3.6 Assignment of Security Responsibility

Within an agency, an individual must be assigned responsibility for each system. This can be accomplished in many ways. In some agencies, the overall responsibility may be delegated to the SAISO. Often, the SAISO is supported by a subnet of security officers assigned to each major component. These security officers may be authorized to address the security requirements for all systems within their domain of authority. Other models may segment this responsibility in other ways based on agency structure and responsibility. The same contact information, as listed under Section 3.3, should be provided for these individuals. Most important is that this responsibility be formalized in writing either in the employee's Position Description or by delegation Memorandum.

3.7 System Operational Status

Indicate one or more of the following for the system's operational status. If more than one status is selected, list which part of the system is covered under each status.

- *Operational* — the system is in production.
- *Under Development* — the system is being designed, developed, or implemented.
- *Undergoing a major modification* — the system is undergoing a major conversion or transition.

If the system is under development or undergoing a major modification, provide information about the methods used to assure that up-front security requirements are included. Include specific controls in the appropriate sections of the plan depending on where the system is in the security life cycle.

3.8 Information System Type

In this section of the plan, indicate whether the system is a major application or general support system. If the system contains minor applications, describe them in the General Description/Purpose section of the plan. If the agency has additional categories of information system types, modify the template to include the other categories.

3.9 General Description/Purpose

Prepare a brief description (one to three paragraphs) of the function and purpose of the system (e.g., economic indicator, network support for an agency, business census data analysis, crop reporting support).

If the system is a general support system, list all applications supported by the general support system. Specify if the application is or is not a major application and include unique name/identifiers, where applicable. Describe each application's function and the information processed. Include a list of user organizations, whether they are internal or external to the system owner's agency.

3.10 System Environment

Provide a brief (one to three paragraphs) general description of the technical system. Include any environmental or technical factors that raise special security concerns, such as use of Personal Digital Assistants, wireless technology, etc. Typically, operational environments are as follows:

- **Standalone or Small Office/Home Office (SOHO)** describes small, informal computer installations that are used for home or business purposes. Standalone encompasses a variety of small-scale environments and devices, ranging from laptops, mobile devices, or home computers, to telecommuting systems, to small businesses and small branch offices of a company.

- **Managed or Enterprise** are typically large agency systems with defined, organized suites of hardware and software configurations, usually consisting of centrally managed workstations and servers protected from the Internet by firewalls and other network security devices.

- **Custom** environments contain systems in which the functionality and degree of security do not fit the other environments. Two typical Custom environments are **Specialized Security-Limited Functionality and Legacy**:

    -- **Specialized Security-Limited Functionality**. A Specialized Security-Limited Functionality environment contains systems and networks at high risk of attack or data exposure, with security taking precedence over functionality. It assumes systems have limited or specialized (not general purpose workstations or systems) functionality in a highly threatened environment such as an outward facing firewall or public web server or whose data content or mission purpose is of such value that aggressive trade-offs in favor of security outweigh the potential negative consequences to other useful system attributes such as legacy applications or interoperability with other systems. A Specialized Security-Limited Functionality environment could be a subset of another environment.

    -- **Legacy**. A Legacy environment contains older systems or applications that may use older, less-secure communication mechanisms. Other machines operating in a Legacy environment may need less restrictive security settings so that they can communicate with legacy systems and applications. A Legacy environment could be a subset of a standalone or managed environment.[16]

---

[16] For a detailed explanation of system environments, see NIST Special Publication 800-70, *Security Configuration Checklists Program for IT Products -- Guidance for Checklists Users and Developers.*

3.11 System Interconnection/Information Sharing

System interconnection is the direct connection of two or more IT systems for the purpose of sharing information resources. System interconnection, if not appropriately protected, may result in a compromise of all connected systems and the data they store, process, or transmit. It is important that system owners, information owners, and management obtain as much information as possible regarding vulnerabilities associated with system interconnections and information sharing. This is essential to selecting the appropriate controls required to mitigate those vulnerabilities. An Interconnection Security Agreement (ISA), Memorandum of Understanding (MOU), or Memorandum of Agreement (MOA) is needed between systems (not between workstations/desktops or publicly accessed systems) that share data that are owned or operated by different organizations. An ISA is not needed with internal agency systems if an agency manages and enforces a rigid system development life cycle, which requires approvals and sign-offs ensuring compliance with security requirements. For additional information on interconnections, see NIST SP 800-47, *Security Guide for Interconnecting Information Technology Systems.*

In this section, for ***each interconnection*** between systems that are owned or operated by different organizations, provide the following information concerning the authorization for the connection to other systems or the sharing of information:

- Name of system;

- Organization;

- Type of interconnection (Internet, Dial-Up, etc.);

- Authorizations for interconnection (MOU/MOA, ISA);

- Date of agreement;

- FIPS 199 Category;

- Certification and accreditation status of system; and

- Name and title of authorizing official(s).

For agencies with numerous interconnections, a table format including the above information may be a good way to present the information.

3.12 Laws, Regulations, and Policies Affecting the System

List any laws, regulations, or policies that establish specific requirements for confidentiality, integrity, or availability of the system and information retained by, transmitted by, or processed by the system. General agency security requirements need not be listed since they mandate security for all systems. Each agency should decide on the level of laws, regulations, and policies to include in the system security plan. Examples might include the Privacy Act of 1974 or a specific statute or regulation concerning the information processed (e.g., tax or census information). If the system processes records subject to the Privacy Act, include the number and title of the Privacy Act system(s) of records and whether the system(s) are used for computer matching activities.

3.13 Security Control Selection

In preparation for documenting how the NIST SP 800-53 security controls for the applicable security control baseline (low-, moderate-, or high impact information systems) are implemented or planned to be implemented, the security controls contained in the baseline should be reviewed and possibly tailored. The scoping guidelines explained in Section 2.5.1 should be used when determining the applicability or tailoring of individual controls. Additionally the controls that are common among numerous systems or within the whole agency should be identified and then documented in the plan. See Section 2.5.3 for guidance on how the common controls should be determined, documented, and coordinated. The process of selecting the appropriate security controls and applying the scoping guidelines to achieve *adequate security*[17] is a multifaceted, risk-based activity involving management and operational personnel within the agency and should be conducted before the security control portion of the plan is written.

- For *low-impact* information systems, an agency must, as a minimum, employ the security controls from the low baseline of security controls defined in NIST SP 800-53 and must ensure that the minimum assurance requirements associated with the low baseline are satisfied.

- For *moderate-impact* information systems, an agency must, as a minimum, employ the security controls from the moderate baseline of security controls defined in NIST SP 800-53 and must ensure that the minimum assurance requirements associated with the moderate baseline are satisfied.

- For *high-impact* information systems, an agency must, as a minimum, employ the security controls from the high baseline of security controls defined in NIST SP 800-53 and must ensure that the minimum assurance requirements associated with the high baseline are satisfied.

3.14 Minimum Security Controls

Now that the security controls have been selected, tailored, and the common controls identified, describe each control. The description should contain 1) the security control title; 2) how the security control is being implemented or planned to be implemented; 3)

---

[17] The Office of Management and Budget (OMB) Circular A-130, Appendix III, defines adequate security as security commensurate with the risk and the magnitude of harm resulting from the loss, misuse, or unauthorized access to or modification of information.

any scoping guidance that has been applied and what type of consideration; and 4) indicate if the security control is a common control and who is responsible for its implementation.

Security controls in the security control catalog (NIST SP 800-53, Appendix F) have a well-defined organization and structure. The security controls are organized into classes and families for ease of use in the control selection and specification process. There are three general classes of security controls (i.e., management, operational, and technical[18]). Each family contains security controls related to the security function of the family. A standardized, two-character identifier is assigned to uniquely identify each control family. Table 2 summarizes the classes and families in the security control catalog and the associated family identifiers.

CLASS	FAMILY	IDENTIFIER
Management	Risk Assessment	RA
Management	Planning	PL
Management	System and Services Acquisition	SA
Management	Certification, Accreditation, and Security Assessments	CA
Operational	Personnel Security	PS
Operational	Physical and Environmental Protection	PE
Operational	Contingency Planning	CP
Operational	Configuration Management	CM
Operational	Maintenance	MA
Operational	System and Information Integrity	SI
Operational	Media Protection	MP
Operational	Incident Response	IR
Operational	Awareness and Training	AT
Technical	Identification and Authentication	IA
Technical	Access Control	AC
Technical	Audit and Accountability	AU
Technical	System and Communications Protection	SC

Table 2: Security Control Class, Family, and Identifier

Security control class designations (i.e., management, operational, and technical) are defined below for clarification in preparation of system security plans.
Management controls focus on the management of the information system and the management of risk for a system. They are techniques and concerns that are normally addressed by management. *Operational controls* address security methods focusing on

---

[18] Security control families in NIST SP 800-53 are associated with one of three security control classes (i.e., management, operational, technical). Families are assigned to their respective classes based on the dominant characteristics of the controls in that family. Many security controls, however, can be logically associated with more than one class. For example, CP-1, the policy and procedures control from the Contingency Planning family, is listed as an operational control but also has characteristics that are consistent with security management as well.

mechanisms primarily implemented and executed by people (as opposed to systems). These controls are put in place to improve the security of a particular system (or group of systems). They often require technical or specialized expertise and often rely upon management activities as well as technical controls. ***Technical controls*** focus on security controls that the computer system executes. The controls can provide automated protection for unauthorized access or misuse, facilitate detection of security violations, and support security requirements for applications and data.

3.15 Completion and Approval Dates

The completion date of the system security plan should be provided. The completion date should be updated whenever the plan is periodically reviewed and updated. When the system is updated, a version number should be added. The system security plan should also contain the date the authorizing official or the designated approving authority approved the plan. Approval documentation, i.e., accreditation letter, approval memorandum, should be on file or attached as part of the plan.

3.16 Ongoing System Security Plan Maintenance

Once the information system security plan is developed, it is important to periodically assess the plan, review any change in system status, functionality, design, etc., and ensure that the plan continues to reflect the correct information about the system. This documentation and its correctness are critical for system certification activity. All plans should be reviewed and updated, if appropriate, at least annually. Some items to include in the review are:

- Change in information system owner;
- Change in information security representative;
- Change in system architecture;
- Change in system status;
- Additions/deletions of system interconnections;
- Change in system scope;
- Change in authorizing official; and
- Change in certification and accreditation status.

Appendix A: Sample Information System Security Plan Template

The following sample has been provided ONLY as one example. Agencies may be using other formats and choose to update those to reflect any existing omissions based on this guidance. This is not a mandatory format; it is recognized that numerous agencies and information security service providers may have developed and implemented various approaches for information system security plan development and presentation to suit their own needs for flexibility.

Information System Security Plan Template

1. Information System Name/Title:
- Unique identifier and name given to the system.

2. Information System Categorization:
- Identify the appropriate FIPS 199 categorization.

	LOW		MODERATE		HIGH

3. Information System Owner:
- Name, title, agency, address, email address, and phone number of person who owns the system.

4. Authorizing Official:
- Name, title, agency, address, email address, and phone number of the senior management official designated as the authorizing official.

5. Other Designated Contacts:
- List other key personnel, if applicable; include their title, address, email address, and phone number.

6. Assignment of Security Responsibility:
- Name, title, address, email address, and phone number of person who is responsible for the security of the system.

7. Information System Operational Status:
- Indicate the operational status of the system. If more than one status is selected, list which part of the system is covered under each status.

	Operational		Under Development		Major Modification

8. Information System Type:
- Indicate if the system is a major application or a general support system. If the system contains minor applications, list them in Section 9. General System Description/Purpose.

	Major Application		General Support System

9. General System Description/Purpose
- Describe the function or purpose of the system and the information processes.

10. System Environment
- Provide a general description of the technical system. Include the primary hardware, software, and communications equipment.

11. System Interconnections/Information Sharing
- List interconnected systems and system identifiers (if appropriate), provide the system, name, organization, system type (major application or general support system), indicate if there is an ISA/MOU/MOA on file, date of agreement to interconnect, FIPS 199 category, C&A status, and the name of the authorizing official.

System Name	Organization	Type	Agreement (ISA/MOU/MOA)	Date	FIPS 199 Category	C&A Status	Auth. Official

12. Related Laws/Regulations/Policies
- List any laws or regulations that establish specific requirements for the confidentiality, integrity, or availability of the data in the system.

13. Minimum Security Controls
Select the appropriate minimum security control baseline (low-, moderate-, high-impact) from NIST SP 800-53, then provide a thorough description of how all the minimum security controls in the applicable baseline are being implemented or planned to be implemented. The description should contain: 1) the security control title; 2) how the security control is being implemented or planned to be implemented; 3) any scoping guidance that has been applied and what type of consideration; and 4) indicate if the security control is a common control and who is responsible for its implementation.

14. Information System Security Plan Completion Date: _____
- Enter the completion date of the plan.

15. Information System Security Plan Approval Date: _____
- Enter the date the system security plan was approved and indicate if the approval documentation is attached or on file.

Appendix B: Glossary

COMMON TERMS AND DEFINITIONS

Accreditation [NIST SP 800-37]	The official management decision given by a senior agency official to authorize operation of an information system and to explicitly accept the risk to agency operations (including mission, functions, image, or reputation), agency assets, or individuals, based on the implementation of an agreed-upon set of security controls.
Accreditation Boundary [NIST SP 800-37]	All components of an information system to be accredited by an authorizing official and excludes separately accredited systems, to which the information system is connected. Synonymous with the term security perimeter defined in CNSS Instruction 4009 and DCID 6/3.
Accrediting Authority	See Authorizing Official.
Adequate Security [OMB Circular A-130, Appendix III]	Security commensurate with the risk and the magnitude of harm resulting from the loss, misuse, or unauthorized access to or modification of information.
Agency	See Executive Agency.
Authentication	Verifying the identity of a user, process, or device, often as a prerequisite to allowing access to resources in an information system.
Authenticity	The property of being genuine and being able to be verified and trusted; confidence in the validity of a transmission, a message, or message originator. See authentication.
Authorize Processing	See Accreditation.
Authorizing Official [NIST SP 800-37]	Official with the authority to formally assume responsibility for operating an information system at an acceptable level of risk to agency operations (including mission, functions, image, or reputation), agency assets, or individuals.
Availability [44 U.S.C., Sec. 3542]	Ensuring timely and reliable access to and use of information.

Certification [NIST SP 800-37]	A comprehensive assessment of the management, operational, and technical security controls in an information system, made in support of security accreditation, to determine the extent to which the controls are implemented correctly, operating as intended, and producing the desired outcome with respect to meeting the security requirements for the system.
Certification Agent [NIST SP 800-37]	The individual, group, or organization responsible for conducting a security certification.
Chief Information Officer [44 U.S.C., Sec. 5125(b)]	Agency official responsible for: (i) Providing advice and other assistance to the head of the executive agency and other senior management personnel of the agency to ensure that information technology is acquired and information resources are managed in a manner that is consistent with laws, executive orders, directives, policies, regulations, and priorities established by the head of the agency; (ii) Developing, maintaining, and facilitating the implementation of a sound and integrated information technology architecture for the agency; and (iii) Promoting the effective and efficient design and operation of all major information resources management processes for the agency, including improvements to work processes of the agency.
Common Security Control [NIST SP 800-37]	Security control that can be applied to one or more agency information systems and has the following properties: (i) the development, implementation, and assessment of the control can be assigned to a responsible official or organizational element (other than the information system owner); and (ii) the results from the assessment of the control can be used to support the security certification and accreditation processes of an agency information system where that control has been applied.
Compensating Security Controls	The management, operational, and technical controls (i.e., safeguards or countermeasures) employed by an organization in lieu of the recommended controls in the low, moderate, or high baselines described in NIST SP 800-53, that provide equivalent or comparable protection for an information system.
Confidentiality [44 U.S.C., Sec. 3542]	Preserving authorized restrictions on information access and disclosure, including means for protecting personal privacy and proprietary information.

Configuration Control [CNSS Inst. 4009]	Process for controlling modifications to hardware, firmware, software, and documentation to ensure that the information system is protected against improper modifications before, during, and after system implementation.
Countermeasures [CNSS Inst. 4009]	Actions, devices, procedures, techniques, or other measures that reduce the vulnerability of an information system. Synonymous with security controls and safeguards.
Executive Agency [41 U.S.C., Sec. 403]	An executive department specified in 5 U.S.C., Sec. 101; a military department specified in 5 U.S.C., Sec. 102; an independent establishment as defined in 5 U.S.C., Sec. 104(1); and a wholly owned Government corporation fully subject to the provisions of 31 U.S.C., Chapter 91.
Federal Enterprise Architecture [FEA Program Management Office]	A business-based framework for government-wide improvement developed by the Office of Management and Budget that is intended to facilitate efforts to transform the federal government to one that is citizen-centered, results-oriented, and market-based.
Federal Information System [40 U.S.C., Sec. 11331]	An information system used or operated by an executive agency, by a contractor of an executive agency, or by another organization on behalf of an executive agency.
General Support System [OMB Circular A-130, Appendix III]	An interconnected set of information resources under the same direct management control that shares common functionality. It normally includes hardware, software, information, data, applications, communications, and people.
High-Impact System	An information system in which at least one security objective (i.e., confidentiality, integrity, or availability) is assigned a FIPS 199 potential impact value of high.
Information Owner [CNSS Inst. 4009]	Official with statutory or operational authority for specified information and responsibility for establishing the controls for its generation, collection, processing, dissemination, and disposal.
Information Resources [44 U.S.C., Sec. 3502]	Information and related resources, such as personnel, equipment, funds, and information technology.

Information Security [44 U.S.C., Sec. 3542]	The protection of information and information systems from unauthorized access, use, disclosure, disruption, modification, or destruction in order to provide confidentiality, integrity, and availability.
Information Security Policy [CNSS Inst. 4009]	Aggregate of directives, regulations, rules, and practices that prescribes how an organization manages, protects, and distributes information.
Information System [44 U.S.C., Sec. 3502] [OMB Circular A-130, Appendix III]	A discrete set of information resources organized for the collection, processing, maintenance, use, sharing, dissemination, or disposition of information.
Information System Owner (or Program Manager) [CNSS Inst. 4009, Adapted]	Official responsible for the overall procurement, development, integration, modification, or operation and maintenance of an information system.
Information System Security Officer [CNSS Inst. 4009, Adapted]	Individual assigned responsibility by the senior agency information security officer, authorizing official, management official, or information system owner for ensuring that the appropriate operational security posture is maintained for an information system or program.
Information Technology [40 U.S.C., Sec. 1401]	Any equipment or interconnected system or subsystem of equipment that is used in the automatic acquisition, storage, manipulation, management, movement, control, display, switching, interchange, transmission, or reception of data or information by the executive agency. For purposes of the preceding sentence, equipment is used by an executive agency if the equipment is used by the executive agency directly or is used by a contractor under a contract with the executive agency which: (i) requires the use of such equipment; or (ii) requires the use, to a significant extent, of such equipment in the performance of a service or the furnishing of a product. The term information technology includes computers, ancillary equipment, software, firmware, and similar procedures, services (including support services), and related resources.

Information Type [FIPS 199]	A specific category of information (e.g., privacy, medical, proprietary, financial, investigative, contractor sensitive, security management) defined by an organization or in some instances, by a specific law, executive order, directive, policy, or regulation.
Integrity [44 U.S.C., Sec. 3542]	Guarding against improper information modification or destruction, and includes ensuring information non-repudiation and authenticity.
Label	See Security Label.
Low-Impact System	An information system in which all three security objectives (i.e., confidentiality, integrity, and availability) are assigned a FIPS 199 potential impact value of low.
Major Application [OMB Circular A-130, Appendix III]	An application that requires special attention to security due to the risk and magnitude of harm resulting from the loss, misuse, or unauthorized access to or modification of the information in the application. Note: All federal applications require some level of protection. Certain applications, because of the information in them, however, require special management oversight and should be treated as major. Adequate security for other applications should be provided by security of the systems in which they operate.
Major Information System [OMB Circular A-130]	An information system that requires special management attention because of its importance to an agency mission; its high development, operating, or maintenance costs; or its significant role in the administration of agency programs, finances, property, or other resources.
Management Controls [NIST SP 800-18]	The security controls (i.e., safeguards or countermeasures) for an information system that focus on the management of risk and the management of information system security.
Media Access Control Address	A hardware address that uniquely identifies each component of an IEEE 802-based network. On networks that do not conform to the IEEE 802 standards but do conform to the OSI Reference Model, the node address is called the Data Link Control (DLC) address.
Minor Application	An application, other than a major application, that requires attention to security due to the risk and magnitude of harm resulting from the loss, misuse, or unauthorized access to or modification of the information in the application. Minor applications are typically included as part of a general support system.
Mobile Code	Software programs or parts of programs obtained from remote information systems, transmitted across a network, and executed on a local information system without explicit installation or execution by the recipient.

Mobile Code Technologies	Software technologies that provide the mechanisms for the production and use of mobile code (e.g., Java, JavaScript, ActiveX, VBScript).
Moderate-Impact System	An information system in which at least one security objective (i.e., confidentiality, integrity, or availability) is assigned a FIPS 199 potential impact value of moderate and no security objective is assigned a FIPS 199 potential impact value of high.
National Security Emergency Preparedness Telecommunications Services	Telecommunications services that are used to maintain a state of readiness or to respond to and manage any event or crisis (local, national, or international) that causes or could cause injury or harm to the population, damage to or loss of property, or degrade or threaten the national security or emergency preparedness posture of the United States.
National Security Information	Information that has been determined pursuant to Executive Order 12958 as amended by Executive Order 13292, or any predecessor order, or by the Atomic Energy Act of 1954, as amended, to require protection against unauthorized disclosure and is marked to indicate its classified status.
National Security System [44 U.S.C., Sec. 3542]	Any information system (including any telecommunications system) used or operated by an agency or by a contractor of an agency, or other organization on behalf of an agency— (i) the function, operation, or use of which involves intelligence activities; involves cryptologic activities related to national security; involves command and control of military forces; involves equipment that is an integral part of a weapon or weapons system; or is critical to the direct fulfillment of military or intelligence missions (excluding a system that is to be used for routine administrative and business applications, for example, payroll, finance, logistics, and personnel management applications); or (ii) is protected at all times by procedures established for information that have been specifically authorized under criteria established by an Executive Order or an Act of Congress to be kept classified in the interest of national defense or foreign policy.
Non-repudiation [CNSS Inst. 4009]	Assurance that the sender of information is provided with proof of delivery and the recipient is provided with proof of the sender's identity, so neither can later deny having processed the information.
Operational Controls [NIST SP 800-18]	The security controls (i.e., safeguards or countermeasures) for an information system that primarily are implemented and executed by people (as opposed to systems).

Plan of Action and Milestones [OMB Memorandum 02-01]	A document that identifies tasks needing to be accomplished. It details resources required to accomplish the elements of the plan, any milestones in meeting the tasks, and scheduled completion dates for the milestones.
Potential Impact [FIPS 199]	The loss of confidentiality, integrity, or availability could be expected to have: (i) a limited adverse effect (FIPS 199 low); (ii) a serious adverse effect (FIPS 199 moderate); or (iii) a severe or catastrophic adverse effect (FIPS 199 high) on organizational operations, organizational assets, or individuals.
Privacy Impact Assessment [OMB Memorandum 03-22]	An analysis of how information is handled: (i) to ensure handling conforms to applicable legal, regulatory, and policy requirements regarding privacy; (ii) to determine the risks and effects of collecting, maintaining, and disseminating information in identifiable form in an electronic information system; and (iii) to examine and evaluate protections and alternative processes for handling information to mitigate potential privacy risks.
Protective Distribution System	Wire line or fiber optic system that includes adequate safeguards and/or countermeasures (e.g., acoustic, electric, electromagnetic, and physical) to permit its use for the transmission of unencrypted information.
Records	The recordings of evidence of activities performed or results achieved (e.g., forms, reports, test results), which serve as a basis for verifying that the organization and the information system are performing as intended. Also used to refer to units of related data fields (i.e., groups of data fields that can be accessed by a program and that contain the complete set of information on particular items).
Remote Access	Access by users (or information systems) communicating external to an information system security perimeter.
Remote Maintenance	Maintenance activities conducted by individuals communicating external to an information system security perimeter.
Risk [NIST SP 800-30]	The level of impact on agency operations (including mission, functions, image, or reputation), agency assets, or individuals resulting from the operation of an information system given the potential impact of a threat and the likelihood of that threat occurring.

Risk Assessment [NIST SP 800-30]	The process of identifying risks to agency operations (including mission, functions, image, or reputation), agency assets, or individuals by determining the probability of occurrence, the resulting impact, and additional security controls that would mitigate this impact. Part of risk management, synonymous with risk analysis, and incorporates threat and vulnerability analyses.
Risk Management [NIST SP 800-30]	The process of managing risks to agency operations (including mission, functions, image, or reputation), agency assets, or individuals resulting from the operation of an information system. It includes risk assessment; cost-benefit analysis; the selection, implementation, and assessment of security controls; and the formal authorization to operate the system. The process considers effectiveness, efficiency, and constraints due to laws, directives, policies, or regulations.
Safeguards [CNSS Inst. 4009, Adapted]	Protective measures prescribed to meet the security requirements (i.e., confidentiality, integrity, and availability) specified for an information system. Safeguards may include security features, management constraints, personnel security, and security of physical structures, areas, and devices. Synonymous with security controls and countermeasures.
Sanitization [CNSS Inst. 4009, Adapted]	Process to remove information from media such that information recovery is not possible. It includes removing all labels, markings, and activity logs.
Scoping Guidance	Provides organizations with specific technology-related, infrastructure-related, public access-related, scalability-related, common security control-related, and risk-related considerations on the applicability and implementation of individual security controls in the control baseline.
Security Category [FIPS 199]	The characterization of information or an information system based on an assessment of the potential impact that a loss of confidentiality, integrity, or availability of such information or information system would have on organizational operations, organizational assets, or individuals.
Security Controls [FIPS 199]	The management, operational, and technical controls (i.e., safeguards or countermeasures) prescribed for an information system to protect the confidentiality, integrity, and availability of the system and its information.
Security Control Baseline	The set of minimum security controls defined for a low-impact, moderate-impact, or high-impact information system.
Security Control Enhancements	Statements of security capability to: (i) build in additional, but related, functionality to a basic control; and/or (ii) increase the strength of a basic control.

Security Impact Analysis [NIST SP 800-37]	The analysis conducted by an agency official, often during the continuous monitoring phase of the security certification and accreditation process, to determine the extent to which changes to the information system have affected the security posture of the system.
Security Label	Explicit or implicit marking of a data structure or output media associated with an information system representing the FIPS 199 security category, or distribution limitations or handling caveats of the information contained therein.
Security Objective	Confidentiality, integrity, or availability.
Security Perimeter	See Accreditation Boundary.
Security Plan	See System Security Plan.
Security Requirements	Requirements levied on an information system that are derived from laws, executive orders, directives, policies, instructions, regulations, or organizational (mission) needs to ensure the confidentiality, integrity, and availability of the information being processed, stored, or transmitted.
Senior Agency Information Security Officer [44 U.S.C., Sec. 3544]	Official responsible for carrying out the Chief Information Officer responsibilities under FISMA and serving as the Chief Information Officer's primary liaison to the agency's authorizing officials, information system owners, and information system security officers.
Spyware	Software that is secretly or surreptitiously installed into an information system to gather information on individuals or organizations without their knowledge.
Subsystem	A major subdivision or component of an information system consisting of information, information technology, and personnel that perform one or more specific functions.
System	See Information System.
System-specific Security Control [NIST SP 800-37]	A security control for an information system that has not been designated as a common security control.
System Security Plan [NIST SP 800-18]	Formal document that provides an overview of the security requirements for the information system and describes the security controls in place or planned for meeting those requirements.

Technical Controls [NIST SP 800-18]	The security controls (i.e., safeguards or countermeasures) for an information system that are primarily implemented and executed by the information system through mechanisms contained in the hardware, software, or firmware components of the system.
Threat [CNSS Inst. 4009, Adapted]	Any circumstance or event with the potential to adversely impact agency operations (including mission, functions, image, or reputation), agency assets, or individuals through an information system via unauthorized access, destruction, disclosure, modification of information, and/or denial of service.
Threat Agent/Source [NIST SP 800-30]	Either: (i) intent and method targeted at the intentional exploitation of a vulnerability; or (ii) a situation and method that may accidentally trigger a vulnerability.
Threat Assessment [CNSS Inst. 4009]	Formal description and evaluation of threat to an information system.
Trusted Path	A mechanism by which a user (through an input device) can communicate directly with the security functions of the information system with the necessary confidence to support the system security policy. This mechanism can only be activated by the user or the security functions of the information system and cannot be imitated by untrusted software.
User [CNSS Inst. 4009]	Individual or (system) process authorized to access an information system.
Vulnerability [CNSS Inst. 4009, Adapted]	Weakness in an information system, system security procedures, internal controls, or implementation that could be exploited or triggered by a threat source.
Vulnerability Assessment [CNSS Inst. 4009]	Formal description and evaluation of the vulnerabilities in an information system.

Appendix C: References

Federal Information Processing Standards Publication 199, *Standards for Security Categorization of Federal Information and Information Systems*, December 2003.

Federal Information Processing Standards Publication 200, *Security Controls for Federal Information System*, (projected for publication February 2006).

Federal Information Security Management Act (P.L. 107-347, Title III), December 2002.

National Institute of Standards and Technology Special Publication 800-26, *Security Self-Assessment Guide for Information Technology Systems,* November 2001.

National Institute of Standards and Technology Special Publication 800-30, *Risk Management Guide for Information Technology Systems,* July 2002.

National Institute of Standards and Technology Special Publication 800-37, *Guide for the Security Certification and Accreditation of Federal Information Systems*, May 2004.

National Institute of Standards and Technology Special Publication 800-47, *Security Guide for Interconnecting Information Technology Systems,* August 2002.

National Institute of Standards and Technology Special Publication 800-53, *Recommended Security Controls for Federal Information Systems,* February 2005.

National Institute of Standards and Technology Special Publication 800-59, *Guideline for Identifying an Information System as a National Security System*, August 2003.

National Institute of Standards and Technology Special Publication 800-60, *Guide for Mapping Types of Information and Information Systems to Security Categories*, June 2004.

National Institute of Standards and Technology Special Publication 800-64, Revision 1, *Security Considerations in the Information System Development Life Cycle*, June 2004.

National Institute of Standards and Technology Special Publication 800-65, *Integrating Security into the Capital Planning and Investment Control Process,* January 2005.

National Institute of Standards and Technology Special Publication 800-70, *Security Configuration Checklists Program for IT Products -- Guidance for Checklists Users and Developers,* May 2005.

Office of Management and Budget, Circular A-130, Appendix III, Transmittal Memorandum #4, *Management of Federal Information Resources*, November 2000.

Following is an excerpt from the book titled "**Cyber-Physical Attack Defenses: Preventing Damage to Buildings and Utilities**", by Luis Ayala. Available at Amazon.com, Barnes & Noble and Books-a-Million.

Hacking into a Building Controls Systems (BCS), Industrial Controls Systems (ICS), and Supervisory Controls and Data Acquisition (SCADA) networks is not the same as breaking into enterprise networks that process information. BCS, ICS and SCADA systems are much more complex. Breaking into a controls system is only a means to an end. The target is not the network itself, it is the equipment being controlled.

A cyber-physical attack represents a weaponization of the Internet.

Although designing a catastrophic cyber-physical attack scenario to exploit a particular physical process requires a solid engineering background and in-depth destructive knowledge of the target controls system (Cyber-Physical Attack Engineering) – you don't need an engineering background to figure out how to turn equipment off.

In addition, a typical ICS contains multiple control loops and sometimes the control loops are nested and/or cascading, so the set point for one loop is based on the process variable output from another loop. Interrupting one process can have a ripple effect through the factory. Supervisory control loops and lower-level loops operate continuously over the duration of a process with cycle times of milliseconds.

A cracker doesn't need to have an engineering degree to figure out that a large change in the setpoint (or process values) on a proportional feedback system will have a larger effect than a small change that would be tolerated based on the sensitivity of the control system and the process. But, even a small change that results in sluggish response in the short-term could have a major effect over a relatively long period of time.

The only saving grace is that a newbie or script kiddie will not thoroughly understand complex manufacturing processes. While a newbie may be able to turn off the lights in the factory, I doubt he would know how to increase the deadband (an interval of a signal domain where no action occurs - the system is 'dead' - i.e. the output is zero) on voltage regulators, or cause repeated activation-deactivation cycles.

Hacking a chemical plant to create a weapon of mass destruction (a Bhopal-style catastrophic failure) for example, requires knowledge of physics, chemistry and engineering, as well as a great deal about how the network is laid out, and a keen understanding of process-aware defensive systems. The most a newbie could hope to do is to turn something off.

A well-qualified attacker (such as a foreign security service) hitting a building or utilities controls network seeks to take control over the equipment. Those crackers understand the equipment they will be controlling. No offense but, most IT guys are not familiar with electrical and mechanical equipment, industrial and manufacturing equipment, or utility equipment, so they wouldn't know how to defend them. That's because they don't know the equipment or processes being controlled.

The same is true of the folks in charge of physical security at these facilities. The typical security guys don't know anything about electrical and mechanical systems, or how computer networks are designed. Let's face it, they don't have the budget or the training to deal with these new threats.

The owner is looking to the facility guys, the IT guys and the security guys to work together to defend their physical plant, and in many cases, these guys aren't even talking to each other. Most of the time, they think cyber-physical security is someone else's responsibility! In essence, "nobody is minding the store". An effective defense against cyber-physical attacks requires procedural safeguards, such as frequent password changes, equipment inspections, random drills, security awareness programs, records retention programs, etc.

So, what is the big deal?

On December 3 1984, in Bhopal, India there was an industrial accident at a pesticide plant that immediately killed at least 3,800 people and caused significant morbidity and premature death for many thousands more. That was only one incident with a release of only 40 tons of methyl isocyanate gas. Of course, this was an accident and not a cyber-physical attack, but it should give you an idea what could happen in a worst-case scenario.

Imagine you wake up in the morning and go the bathroom. You turn on the faucet and nothing happens. You go back to the bedroom and the clock is flashing 12:00. You hit the power button on the TV remote and nothing happens. It's a little warm in the house but the air conditioning doesn't work. Then you realize that though the sun is out and it's a normal weekday, you don't hear any cars going by. You go outside to your car and it won't start – even the radio doesn't work. The cell phone has no signal and won't stay on when you power up. The toaster doesn't heat up and you have to light the gas stove with a match. It's a nice day so you walk to work and notice a line outside the supermarket, but the doors are locked. You ask why they don't open up and they say there is no power to run the cash registers. Even their backup generator won't start. None of the traffic lights work, but there are no cars on the road anyway. This is a cyber-physical attack that affects all utilities, and many electronic devices.

Or, imagine you've been waiting for months to find a kidney donor and the day you go in for a kidney transplant, the hospital is attacked and the refrigeration equipment that holds human organs is hacked. A malicious attacker changed the temperature setting of the refrigerators overnight, or cut the power entirely. All human organs were lost. Yes, these systems are designed with alarms that send messages to beepers and email, but a determined attacker can defeat those alarms.

Another example is what actually happened at a Chrysler assembly plant. An attacker shut down one auto plant with a worm that quickly spread to all other Chrysler plants, idling 50,000 workers. These were professionally-installed industrial control networks with firewalls and safety features. I suspect they were protected in much the same way that many enterprise networks are protected today.

The bad news is that crackers are getting better at what they do. In the good old days, an attacker would use a virus or worm to take over your computer. Nowadays they can attack your computer without loading any files at all. That's because all the files they need to take over are already loaded on your computer. That's called a Fileless Cyber-Attack. All they need to do is trick you into giving them permission to access those files. Anti-virus software has gotten very good at detecting and stopping a computer virus. Attackers find it much easier to fool a human using social engineering.

In order for you to begin to understand what is going through the mind of someone trying to break into your computer network, I include a lot of Hackerspeak, or Leet-speak in this book. See the definitions a little further on. This should give you some insight into the mind of a hacker.

This book was written to help Owners, Architects, Engineers, and facilities and infrastructure maintenance personnel understand the vulnerability of SCADA systems, building controls systems, and industrial controls systems to cyber-physical attack. The book includes simple descriptions of the vulnerabilities (attack vectors) of automated equipment controls common to buildings, industry and utilities. The book also lists the different types of cyber-physical attacks discovered. It is a handy desk reference for Architects, Engineers, Building Managers, Students, Researchers and Consultants interested in preventing cyber-physical attacks. Remember, a "hacker" and a "cracker" are two different meanings so please stop referring to hackers as bad guys.

The price of connectivity is less security. The more connected a device is, the less secure it will be.

7. Monitor the Process Equipment Looking for Anomalies

It is probably easier to detect a cyber-physical attack (when it occurs) by looking at how the equipment is operating than it is to detect subtle software anomalies or dropped packets. Although boiler water temperature and pressure rising dangerous levels doesn't necessarily signal that a cyber-physical attack is underway, it could be an attack. Don't assume it isn't a cyber-attack out of hand. Look for signs that the controls have been manipulated. Compare what the computer says is happening with what the equipment is actually doing. Remember, a sneaky attacker will change the setpoints higher than normal so the computer will not know something is wrong.

Malicious attackers are more likely to use the process control systems to make equipment "misbehave" while appearing to operate normally. At the Iranian nuclear plant, Stuxnet manipulated the calibration systems so the plant workers didn't see the real pressure readings that would have flagged the problems with the devices early on. Had the workers manually checked the equipment itself frequently, they would have noticed the discrepancy.

A malicious attacker would schedule his attack when it would be less likely to be detected or when it could do the most damage. Startup and shutdown of a process plant are the two most dangerous operational modes of the plant. A well-qualified attacker would know the planned startup sequence of operations and manipulate the amount of heat or the flow of chemicals to corrupt the process and damage the hardware.

For example, industrial distillation is typically performed in large, vertical cylindrical columns known as distillation towers or distillation columns. The amount of heat entering a distillation column is a crucial operating parameter, addition of excess or insufficient heat to the column can lead to foaming, weeping, entrainment, or flooding. If the column contains liquid during pressuring, excessive vapor flows will cause flooding and gas lifting of the liquid, resulting in liquid discharge into relief header and damage the column internals.

The information in this NIST title directly addresses the concerns I articulated in my Cyber-Physical Attack Defenses book. By implementing the attached standard, hopefully your system can survive an attempted cyber-physical attack.

Luis Ayala

CyberSecurity Standards Library™

NIST SP 500-288	Specification for WS-Biometric Devices (WS-BD)
NIST SP 500-291 V2	NIST Cloud Computing Standards Roadmap
NIST SP 500-292	NIST Cloud Computing Reference Architecture
NIST SP 500-293 V1 & V2	US Government Cloud Computing Technology Roadmap
NIST SP 500-293 V3	US Government Cloud Computing Technology Roadmap
NIST SP 500-299	NIST Cloud Computing Security Reference Architecture
NIST SP 500-304	Data Format for the Interchange of Fingerprint, Facial & Other Biometric Information
NIST SP 800-1	Bibliography of Selected Computer Security Publications January 1980-October 1989
NIST SP 800-12 R1	An Introduction to Information Security
NIST SP 800-13	Telecommunications Security Guidelines for Telecommunications Management Network
NIST SP 800-14	Generally Accepted Principles and Practices for Securing Information Technology Systems
NIST SP 800-15 V1	Minimum Interoperability Specification for PKI Components (MISPC)
NIST SP 800-16 R1	A Role-Based Model for Federal Information Technology/Cybersecurity Training
NIST SP 800-17	Modes of Operation Validation System (MOVS): Requirements and Procedures
NIST SP 800-18 R1	Developing Security Plans for Federal Information Systems
NIST SP 800-19	Mobile Agent Security
NIST SP 800-20	Modes of Operation Validation System for the Triple Data Encryption Algorithm
NIST SP 800-22 R1a	A Statistical Test Suite for Random and Pseudorandom Number Generators for Cryptographic Applications
NIST SP 800-23	Guidelines to Federal Organizations on Security Assurance and Acquisition/Use of Tested/Evaluated Products
NIST SP 800-24	PBX Vulnerability Analysis - Finding Holes in Your PBX Before Someone Else Does
NIST SP 800-25	Federal Agency Use of Public Key Technology for Digital Signatures and Authentication
NIST SP 800-27 Rev A	Engineering Principles for Information Technology Security (A Baseline for Achieving Security)
NIST SP 800-28	Guidelines on Active Content and Mobile Code
NIST SP 800-29	A Comparison of the Security Requirements for Cryptographic Modules in FIPS 140-1 and FIPS 140-2
NIST SP 800-30	Guide for Conducting Risk Assessments
NIST SP 800-31	Intrusion Detection Systems
NIST SP 800-32	Public Key Technology and the Federal PKI Infrastructure
NIST SP 800-33	Underlying Technical Models for Information Technology Security
NIST SP 800-34 R1	Contingency Planning Guide for Federal Information Systems
NIST SP 800-35	Guide to Information Technology Security Services
NIST SP 800-36	Guide to Selecting Information Technology Security Products
NIST SP 800-37 R1	Applying Risk Management Framework to Federal Information
NIST SP 800-38	Recommendation for Block Cipher Modes of Operation
NIST SP 800-38A Addendum	Block Cipher Modes of Operation: Three Variants of Ciphertext Stealing for CBC Mode
NIST SP 800-38B	Block Cipher Modes of Operation: The CMAC Mode for Authentication
NIST SP 800-38C	Block Cipher Modes of Operation: The CCM Mode for Authentication and Confidentiality
NIST SP 800-38D	Block Cipher Modes of Operation: Galois/Counter Mode (GCM) and GMAC
NIST SP 800-38E	Block Cipher Modes of Operation: The XTS-AES Mode for Confidentiality on Storage Devices
NIST SP 800-38F	Block Cipher Modes of Operation: Methods for Key Wrapping
NIST SP 800-38G	Block Cipher Modes of Operation: Methods for Format-Preserving Encryption
NIST SP 800-39	Managing Information Security Risk
NIST SP 800-40 R3	Guide to Enterprise Patch Management Technologies
NIST SP 800-41	Guidelines on Firewalls and Firewall Policy
NIST SP 800-43	Systems Administration Guidance for Securing Microsoft Windows 2000 Professional System
NIST SP 800-44 V2	Guidelines on Securing Public Web Servers
NIST SP 800-45 V2	Guidelines on Electronic Mail Security
NIST SP 800-46 R2	Guide to Enterprise Telework, Remote Access, and Bring Your Own Device (BYOD) Security
NIST SP 800-47	Security Guide for Interconnecting Information Technology Systems
NIST SP 800-48	Guide to Securing Legacy IEEE 802.11 Wireless Networks
NIST SP 800-49	Federal S/MIME V3 Client Profile
NIST SP 800-50	Building an Information Technology Security Awareness and Training Program
NIST SP 800-51 R1	Guide to Using Vulnerability Naming Schemes
NIST SP 800-52 R1	Guidelines for the Selection, Configuration, and Use of Transport Layer Security (TLS) Implementations
NIST SP 800-53 R5	Security and Privacy Controls for Information Systems and Organizations
NIST SP 800-53A R4	Assessing Security and Privacy Controls
NIST SP 800-54	Border Gateway Protocol Security
NIST SP 800-55 R1	Performance Measurement Guide for Information Security
NIST SP 800-56A R3	Pair-Wise Key-Establishment Schemes Using Discrete Logarithm Cryptography
NIST SP 56B R 1	Recommendation for Pair-Wise Key-Establishment Schemes Using Integer Factorization Cryptography
NIST SP 800-56C R1	Recommendation for Key-Derivation Methods in Key-Establishment Schemes - Draft
NIST SP 800-57 R4	Recommendation for Key Management
NIST SP 800-58	Security Considerations for Voice Over IP Systems
NIST SP 800-59	Guideline for Identifying an Information System as a National Security System
NIST SP 800-60	Guide for Mapping Types of Information and Information Systems to Security Categories
NIST SP 800-61 R2	Computer Security Incident Handling Guide
NIST SP 800-63-3	Digital Identity Guidelines
NIST SP 800-63a	Digital Identity Guidelines - Enrollment and Identity Proofing
NIST SP 800-63b	Digital Identity Guidelines - Authentication and Lifecycle Management
NIST SP 800-63c	Digital Identity Guidelines- Federation and Assertions
NIST SP 800-64 R2	Security Considerations in the System Development Life Cycle

Click on a title to obtain a printed copy of these standards at Amazon.com
Copyright © 2017 4th Watch Publishing

CyberSecurity Standards Library™

NIST SP 800-65	Integrating IT Security into the Capital Planning and Investment Control Process
NIST SP 800-66	Implementing the Health Insurance Portability and Accountability Act (HIPAA) Security Rule
NIST SP 800-67 R2	Recommendation for Triple Data Encryption Algorithm (TDEA) Block Cipher - Draft
NIST SP 800-68 R1	Guide to Securing Microsoft Windows XP Systems for IT Professionals: A NIST Security Configuration Checklist
NIST SP 800-69	Guidance for Securing Microsoft Windows XP Home Edition: A NIST Security Configuration Checklist
NIST SP 800-70 R4	National Checklist Program for IT Products
NIST SP 800-72	Guidelines on PDA Forensics
NIST SP 800-73-4	Interfaces for Personal Identity Verification
NIST SP 800-76-2	Biometric Specifications for Personal Identity Verification
NIST SP 800-77	Guide to IPsec VPNs
NIST SP 800-78-4	Cryptographic Algorithms and Key Sizes for Personal Identity Verification
NIST SP 800-79-2	Authorization of Personal Identity Verification Card Issuers (PCI) and Derived PIV Credential Issuers (DPCI)
NIST SP 800-81-2	Secure Domain Name System (DNS) Deployment Guide
NIST SP 800-82 R2	Guide to Industrial Control Systems (ICS) Security
NIST SP 800-83	Guide to Malware Incident Prevention and Handling for Desktops and Laptops
NIST SP 800-84	Guide to Test, Training, and Exercise Programs for IT Plans and Capabilities
NIST SP 800-85A-4 PIV	Card Application and Middleware Interface Test Guidelines
NIST SP 800-85B-4 PIV	Data Model Test Guidelines - Draft
NIST SP 800-86	Guide to Integrating Forensic Techniques into Incident Response
NIST SP 800-87 R1	Codes for Identification of Federal and Federally-Assisted Organizations
NIST SP 800-88 R1	Guidelines for Media Sanitization
NIST SP 800-89	Recommendation for Obtaining Assurances for Digital Signature Applications
NIST SP 800-90A R1	Random Number Generation Using Deterministic Random Bit Generators
NIST SP 800-90B	Recommendation for the Entropy Sources Used for Random Bit Generation
NIST SP 800-90C	Recommendation for Random Bit Generator (RBG) Constructions - 2nd Draft
NIST SP 800-92	Guide to Computer Security Log Management
NIST SP 800-94	Guide to Intrusion Detection and Prevention Systems (IDPS)
NIST SP 800-95	Guide to Secure Web Services
NIST SP 800-97	Establishing Wireless Robust Security Networks: A Guide to IEEE 802.11i
NIST SP 800-98	Guidelines for Securing Radio Frequency Identification (RFID) Systems
NIST SP 800-100	Information Security Handbook: A Guide for Managers
NIST SP 800-101 R1	Guidelines on Mobile Device Forensics
NIST SP 800-102	Recommendation for Digital Signature Timeliness
NIST SP 800-106	Randomized Hashing for Digital Signatures
NIST SP 800-107 R1	Recommendation for Applications Using Approved Hash Algorithms
NIST SP 800-108	Recommendation for Key Derivation Using Pseudorandom Functions
NIST SP 800-111	Guide to Storage Encryption Technologies for End User Devices
NIST SP 800-113	Guide to SSL VPNs
NIST SP 800-114 R1	User's Guide to Telework and Bring Your Own Device (BYOD) Security
NIST SP 800-115	Technical Guide to Information Security Testing and Assessment
NIST SP 800-116	A Recommendation for the Use of PIV Credentials in PACS - Draft
NIST SP 800-117 V1.2	Guide to Adopting and Using the Security Content Automation Protocol (SCAP) - Draft
NIST SP 800-119	Guidelines for the Secure Deployment of IPv6
NIST SP 800-120	Recommendation for EAP Methods Used in Wireless Network Access Authentication
NIST SP 800-121 R2	Guide to Bluetooth Security
NIST SP 800-122	Guide to Protecting the Confidentiality of Personally Identifiable Information
NIST SP 800-123	Guide to General Server Security
NIST SP 800-124 R1	Managing the Security of Mobile Devices in the Enterprise
NIST SP 800-125 (A & B)	Secure Virtual Network Configuration for Virtual Machine (VM) Protection
NIST SP 800-126 R3	Technical Specification for the Security Content Automation Protocol (SCAP)
NIST SP 800-126A	SCAP 1.3 Component Specification 3 Version Updates
NIST SP 800-127	Guide to Securing WiMAX Wireless Communications
NIST SP 800-128	Guide for Security-Focused Configuration Management of Information Systems
NIST SP 800-130	A Framework for Designing Cryptographic Key Management Systems
NIST SP 800-131A R1	Transitions: Recommendation for Transitioning the Use of Cryptographic Algorithms and Key Lengths
NIST SP 800-132	Recommendation for Password-Based Key Derivation - Part 1: Storage Applications
NIST SP 800-133	Recommendation for Cryptographic Key Generation
NIST SP 800-135 R1	Recommendation for Existing Application-Specific Key Derivation Functions
NIST SP 800-137	Information Security Continuous Monitoring (ISCM)
NIST SP 800-142	Practical Combinatorial Testing
NIST SP 800-144	Guidelines on Security and Privacy in Public Cloud Computing
NIST SP 800-145	The NIST Definition of Cloud Computing
NIST SP 800-146	Cloud Computing Synopsis and Recommendations
NIST SP 800-147	BIOS Protection Guidelines & BIOS Integrity Measurement Guidelines
NIST SP 800-147B	BIOS Protection Guidelines for Servers
NIST SP 800-150	Guide to Cyber Threat Information Sharing
NIST SP 800-152	A Profile for U.S. Federal Cryptographic Key Management Systems
NIST SP 800-153	Guidelines for Securing Wireless Local Area Networks (WLANs)
NIST SP 800-154	Guide to Data-Centric System Threat Modeling

Click on a title to obtain a printed copy of these standards at Amazon.com

CyberSecurity Standards Library™

NIST SP 800-155	BIOS Integrity Measurement Guidelines
NIST SP 800-156	Representation of PIV Chain-of-Trust for Import and Export
NIST SP 800-157	Guidelines for Derived Personal Identity Verification (PIV) Credentials
NIST SP 800-160	Systems Security Engineering
NIST SP 800-161	Supply Chain Risk Management Practices for Federal Information Systems and Organizations
NIST SP 800-162	Guide to Attribute Based Access Control (ABAC) Definition and Considerations
NIST SP 800-163	Vetting the Security of Mobile Applications
NIST SP 800-164	Guidelines on Hardware- Rooted Security in Mobile Devices Draft
NIST SP 800-166	Derived PIV Application and Data Model Test Guidelines
NIST SP 800-167	Guide to Application Whitelisting
NIST SP 800-168	Approximate Matching: Definition and Terminology
NIST SP 800-171 R1	Protecting Controlled Unclassified Information in Nonfederal Systems
NIST SP 800-175 (A & B)	Guideline for Using Cryptographic Standards in the Federal Government
NIST SP 800-177 R1	Trustworthy Email
NIST SP 800-178	Comparison of Attribute Based Access Control (ABAC) Standards for Data Service Applications
NIST SP 800-179	Guide to Securing Apple OS X 10.10 Systems for IT Professional
NIST SP 800-180	NIST Definition of Microservices, Application Containers and System Virtual Machines
NIST SP 800-181	National Initiative for Cybersecurity Education (NICE) Cybersecurity Workforce Framework
NIST SP 800-183	Networks of 'Things'
NIST SP 800-184	Guide for Cybersecurity Event Recovery
NIST SP 800-185	SHA-3 Derived Functions: cSHAKE, KMAC, TupleHash and ParallelHash
NIST SP 800-187	Guide to LTE Security - Draft
NIST SP 800-188	De-Identifying Government Datasets - (2nd Draft)
NIST SP 800-190	Application Container Security Guide
NIST SP 800-191	The NIST Definition of Fog Computing
NIST SP 800-192	Verification and Test Methods for Access Control Policies/Models
NIST SP 800-193	Platform Firmware Resiliency Guidelines
NIST SP 1800-1	Securing Electronic Health Records on Mobile Devices
NIST SP 1800-2	Identity and Access Management for Electric Utilities 1800-2a & 1800-2b
NIST SP 1800-2	Identity and Access Management for Electric Utilities 1800-2c
NIST SP 1800-3	Attribute Based Access Control NIST 1800-3a & 3b
NIST SP 1800-3	Attribute Based Access Control NIST 1800-3c Chapters 1 - 6
NIST SP 1800-3	Attribute Based Access Control NIST1800-3c Chapters 7 - 10
NIST SP 1800-4a & 4b	Mobile Device Security: Cloud and Hybrid Builds
NIST SP 1800-4c	Mobile Device Security: Cloud and Hybrid Builds
NIST SP 1800-5	IT Asset Management: Financial Services
NIST SP 1800-6	Domain Name Systems-Based Electronic Mail Security
NIST SP 1800-7	Situational Awareness for Electric Utilities
NIST SP 1800-8	Securing Wireless Infusion Pumps
NIST SP 1800-9a & 9b	Access Rights Management for the Financial Services Sector
NIST SP 1800-9c	Access Rights Management for the Financial Services Sector - How To Guide
NIST SP 1800-11a & 11b	Data Integrity Recovering from Ransomware and Other Destructive Events
NIST SP 1800-11c	Data Integrity Recovering from Ransomware and Other Destructive Events - How To Guide
NIST SP 1800-12	Derived Personal Identity Verification (PIV) Credentials
NISTIR 7100	PDA Forensic Tools: An Overview and Analysis
NISTIR 7188	Specification for the Extensible Configuration Checklist Description Format (XCCDF)
NISTIR 7200	Proximity Beacons and Mobile Device Authentication: An Overview and Implementation
NISTIR 7206	Smart Cards and Mobile Device Authentication: An Overview and Implementation
NISTIR 7250	Cell Phone Forensic Tools: An Overview and Analysis
NISTIR 7275 V1.1	Specification for the Extensible Configuration Checklist Description Format (XCCDF)
NISTIR 7275 R4 V1.2	Specification for the Extensible Configuration Checklist Description Format (XCCDF)
NISTIR 7284	Personal Identity Verification Card Management Report
NISTIR 7290	Fingerprint Identification and Mobile Handheld Devices: An Overview and Implementation
NISTIR 7298 R2	Glossary of Key Information Security Terms
NISTIR 7316	Assessment of Access Control Systems
NISTIR 7337	Personal Identity Verification Demonstration Summary
NISTIR 7358	Program Review for Information Security Management Assistance (PRISMA)
NISTIR 7359	Information Security Guide for Government Executives
NISTIR 7387	Cell Phone Forensic Tools: An Overview and Analysis Update
NISTIR 7435	The Common Vulnerability Scoring System (CVSS) and Its Applicability to Federal Agency Systems
NISTIR 7452	Secure Biometric Match-on-Card Feasibility Report
NISTIR 7497	Security Architecture Design Process for Health Information Exchanges (HIEs)
NISTIR 7502	The Common Configuration Scoring System (CCSS): Metrics for Software Security Configuration Vulnerabilities
NISTIR 7511 R4 V1.2	Security Content Automation Protocol (SCAP) Version 1.2 Validation Program Test Requirements
NISTIR 7516	Forensic Filtering of Cell Phone Protocols
NISTIR 7539	Symmetric Key Injection onto Smart Cards
NISTIR 7551	A Threat Analysis on UOCAVA Voting Systems
NISTIR 7559	Forensics Web Services (FWS)
NISTIR 7564	Directions in Security Metrics Research
NISTIR 7581	System and Network Security Acronyms and Abbreviations

Click on a title to obtain a printed copy of these standards at Amazon.com

CyberSecurity Standards Library™

NISTIR 7601	Framework for Emergency Response Officials (ERO)
NISTIR 7611	Use of ISO/IEC 24727
NISTIR 7617	Mobile Forensic Reference Materials: A Methodology and Reification
NISTIR 7621 R1	Small Business Information Security: The Fundamentals
NISTIR 7622	Notional Supply Chain Risk Management Practices for Federal Information Systems
NISTIR 7628 R1 Vol 1	Guidelines for Smart Grid Cybersecurity - Architecture, and High-Level Requirements
NISTIR 7628 R1 Vol 2	Guidelines for Smart Grid Cybersecurity - Privacy and the Smart Grid
NISTIR 7628 R1 Vol 3	Guidelines for Smart Grid Cybersecurity - Supportive Analyses and References
NISTIR 7658	Guide to SIMfill Use and Development
NISTIR 7676	Maintaining and Using Key History on Personal Identity Verification (PIV) Cards
NISTIR 7682	Information System Security Best Practices for UOCAVA-Supporting Systems
NISTIR 7692 V2	Specification for the Open Checklist Interactive Language (OCIL)
NISTIR 7693	Specification for Asset Identification 1.1
NISTIR 7694	Specification for the Asset Reporting Format 1.1
NISTIR 7696 V2.3	Common Platform Enumeration: Name Matching Specification
NISTIR 7697 V2.3	Common Platform Enumeration: Dictionary Specification
NISTIR 7698 V2.3	Common Platform Enumeration: Applicability Language Specification
NISTIR 7711	Security Best Practices for the Electronic Transmission of Election Materials for UOCAVA Voters
NISTIR 7756	CAESARS Framework Extension: An Enterprise Continuous Monitoring Technical Refer
NISTIR 7764	Status Report on the Second Round of the SHA-3 Cryptographic Hash Algorithm Competition
NISTIR 7770	Security Considerations for Remote Electronic UOCAVA Voting
NISTIR 7771 V2	Conformance Test Architecture for Biometric Data Interchange Formats - Beta
NISTIR 7773	An Application of Combinatorial Methods to Conformance Testing for Document Object Model Events
NISTIR 7788	Security Risk Analysis of Enterprise Networks Using Probabilistic Attack Graphs
NISTIR 7791	Conformance Test Architecture and Test Suite for ANSI/NIST-ITL 1-2007
NISTIR 7799	Continuous Monitoring Reference Model, Workflow, and Specifications - Draft
NISTIR 7800	Applying the Continuous Monitoring Technical Reference Model to the Asset, Configuration, and Vulnerability Management Domains - Draft
NISTIR 7823	Advanced Metering Infrastructure Smart Meter Upgradeability Test Framework
NISTIR 7874	Guidelines for Access Control System Evaluation Metrics
NISTIR 7904	Trusted Geolocation in the Cloud: Proof of Concept Implementation
NISTIR 7924	Reference Certificate Policy
NISTIR 7987	Policy Machine: Features, Architecture, and Specification
NISTIR 8006	NIST Cloud Computing Forensic Science Challenges
NISTIR 8011 Vol 1	Automation Support for Security Control Assessments
NISTIR 8011 Vol 2	Automation Support for Security Control Assessments
NISTIR 8040	Measuring the Usability and Security of Permuted Passwords on Mobile Platforms
NISTIR 8053	De-Identification of Personal Information
NISTIR 8054	NSTIC Pilots: Catalyzing the Identity Ecosystem
NISTIR 8055	Derived Personal Identity Verification (PIV) Credentials (DPC) Proof of Concept Research
NISTIR 8060	Guidelines for the Creation of Interoperable Software Identification (SWID) Tags
NISTIR 8062	Introduction to Privacy Engineering and Risk Management in Federal Systems
NISTIR 8074 Vol 1 & Vol 2	Strategic U.S. Government Engagement in International Standardization to Achieve U.S. Objectives for Cybersecurity
NISTIR 8080	Usability and Security Considerations for Public Safety Mobile Authentication
NISTIR 8089	An Industrial Control System Cybersecurity Performance Testbed
NISTIR 8112	Attribute Metadata - Draft
NISTIR 8135	Identifying and Categorizing Data Types for Public Safety Mobile Applications
NISTIR 8138	Vulnerability Description Ontology (VDO)
NISTIR 8144	Assessing Threats to Mobile Devices & Infrastructure
NISTIR 8151	Dramatically Reducing Software Vulnerabilities
NISTIR 8170	The Cybersecurity Framework
NISTIR 8176	Security Assurance Requirements for Linux Application Container Deployments
NISTIR 8179	Criticality Analysis Process Model
NISTIR 8183	Cybersecurity Framework Manufacturing Profile
NISTIR 8192	Enhancing Resilience of the Internet and Communications Ecosystem
Whitepaper	Cybersecurity Framework Manufacturing Profile
Whitepaper	NIST Framework for Improving Critical Infrastructure Cybersecurity
Whitepaper	Challenging Security Requirements for US Government Cloud Computing Adoption
FIPS PUBS 140-2	Security Requirements for Cryptographic Modules
FIPS PUBS 140-2 Annex A	Approved Security Functions
FIPS PUBS 140-2 Annex B	Approved Protection Profiles
FIPS PUBS 140-2 Annex C	Approved Random Number Generators
FIPS PUBS 140-2 Annex D	Approved Key Establishment Techniques
FIPS PUBS 180-4	Secure Hash Standard (SHS)
FIPS PUBS 186-4	Digital Signature Standard (DSS)
FIPS PUBS 197	Advanced Encryption Standard (AES)
FIPS PUBS 198-1	The Keyed-Hash Message Authentication Code (HMAC)
FIPS PUBS 199	Standards for Security Categorization of Federal Information and Information Systems
FIPS PUBS 200	Minimum Security Requirements for Federal Information and Information Systems

Click on a title to obtain a printed copy of these standards at Amazon.com

CyberSecurity Standards Library™

FIPS PUBS 201-2 Personal Identity Verification (PIV) of Federal Employees and Contractors
FIPS PUBS 202 SHA-3 Standard: Permutation-Based Hash and Extendable-Output Functions

DHS Study DHS Study on Mobile Device Security

OMB A-130 / FISMA OMB A-130/Federal Information Security Modernization Act

DoD
UFC 3-430-11 Boiler Control Systems
UFC 4-010-06 Cybersecurity of Facility-Related Control Systems
FC 4-141-05N Navy and Marine Corps Industrial Control Systems Monitoring Stations
MIL-HDBK-232A RED/BLACK Engineering-Installation Guidelines
MIL-HDBK 1195 Radio Frequency Shielded Enclosures
TM 5-601 Supervisory Control and Data Acquisition (SCADA) Systems for C4ISR Facilities
ESTCP Facility-Related Control Systems Cybersecurity Guideline
ESTCP Facility-Related Control Systems Ver 4.0
DoD Self-Assessing Security Vulnerabilities & Risks of Industrial Controls
DoD Program Manager's Guidebook for Integrating the Cybersecurity Risk Management Framework (RMF) into the System Acquisition Lifecycle
DoD Advanced Cyber Industrial Control System Tactics, Techniques, and Procedures (ACI TTP)

NERC
NERC CIP 002-5.1 Cyber Security — BES Cyber System Categorization
NERC CIP 003-6 Cyber Security — Security Management Controls
NERC CIP 003-7(i) Cyber Security — Security Management Controls
NERC CIP 004-6 Cyber Security — Personnel & Training
NERC CIP 005-5 Cyber Security — Electronic Security Perimeter(s)
NERC CIP 006-6 Cyber Security — Physical Security of BES Cyber Systems
NERC CIP 007-6 Cyber Security — Systems Security Management
NERC CIP 008-5 Cyber Security — Incident Reporting and Response Planning
NERC CIP 009-6 Cyber Security — Recovery Plans for BES Cyber Systems
NERC CIP 010-2 Cyber Security — Configuration Change Management and Vulnerability
NERC CIP 011-2 Cyber Security — Information Protection
NERC CIP 014-2 Physical Security

www.ingramcontent.com/pod-product-compliance
Lightning Source LLC
Chambersburg PA
CBHW060442060326
40690CB00019B/4295